THE TRUTH IS
STILL OUT THERE

THIRTY YEARS
OF THE (X) FILES

THE TRUTH IS
STILL OUT THERE

THIRTY YEARS
OF THE (X) FILES

BETHAN JONES

The Truth Is Still Out There: Thirty Years of The X-Files
©2023 Bethan Jones

Cover design by Peter Bellingham
peterbellinghamillustration.com
Edited by David Bushman
Book designed by Scott Ryan
Back cover photo courtesy of Twentieth Century Fox
Author photo by Sarah Jones
Published in the USA by Fayetteville Mafia Press
Columbus, Ohio

Contact Information
Email: FayettevilleMafiaPress@gmail.com
Website: TuckerDSPress.com
Twitter: @FMPBooks
Instagram: @Fayettevillemafiapress
ISBN: 9781949024500
eBook ISBN: 9781949024517

*This book is dedicated to the memory of Ted Millington, who
encouraged me to write,
and my grandparents, who would be so proud.*

CONTENTS

SECTION FOUR - DENY EVERYTHING

Preface

I'm writing this book in my office, drinking tea out of an *X-Files* mug with an "I Want To Believe" mouse mat next to my keyboard. Directly behind me, a cardboard cutout of Mulder and Scully rests against the wall, towering above several fan-made *X-Files* cushions (two of which are owls in the shape of Mulder and Scully). If I look to my right, I can see the Abducted Smoking Alien sculpture from "Jose Chung's 'From Outer Space,'" various boxed PALZ *X-Files* figures, and the 2016 Diamond Select Mulder and Scully action figures (both boxed). To my left, I have various academic books written about the series, dotted among other books about fan cultures, cult television, and reboots; the full set of Waller Customs *X-Files* Lego figures, and a screen-used prop spike from "Darkness Falls" (a fortieth-birthday present from my sister). In an alcove in my study, I have more shelving units and bookcases filled with *X-Files*-related memorabilia and merchandise. Original Topps comics share shelf space with copies of *SFX* magazine and *Radio Times* that feature articles on the show. Clippings from newspapers and magazines sit in a cardboard folder that sits on top of a binder containing the Topps trading cards. The original PS1 game is on a shelf along with copies of the Unrestricted Access PC game, the VHS trivia game, and the 2015 IDW board game, next to a shelf containing the *Fight the Future* VHS Special

Collectors Edition, the *Fight the Future* lunchbox, and the *Fight the Future* action figure set. Those in turn are next to a shelf containing a basketball signed by David Duchovny that was given as a crew gift at the end of season five, which is below a shelf containing *The X-Files* Funko Pop figures and a clapper board signed by Chris Carter during the season ten revival. And that's to say nothing of the various T-shirts, jackets, bags, and caps that are in my wardrobe or the posters and fan art that adorn my walls.

This collection, amassed over the last twenty-six years, is a testament to how the show has helped define me and my life. My academic career was shaped by my involvement in the fandom: my third-year philosophy dissertation looked at reality and fiction in contemporary film and television, and I used "Milagro" and "Jose Chung's 'From Outer Space'" as my case studies. My master's degree involved writing about fan fiction—something I've done since the days of the BBC Cult message boards—and my PhD research involved surveying thousands of fans about the *X-Files* revival. Without *The X-Files*, my life would be very different. But I could never have seen that when the show began.

The first season of *The X-Files* aired in 1994 here in the UK, when I was twelve. And I didn't watch it. As a kid, I was already interested in the paranormal and read books about ghosts and the Loch Ness Monster, so I was skeptical about this new series. I read books by Isaac Asimov and Arthur C. Clarke, inspired by my grandad's library, and I was determined to be a parapsychologist when I grew up. This new series was bound to be silly and inferior and poke fun at those of us genuinely interested in the paranormal. I wasn't going to watch it. But my stepfather did, and one evening I walked into the living room while it was on. I was hooked. I can't tell you why—it might have been the chemistry between David Duchovny and Gillian Anderson; it might have been that it was nothing like any other show I'd seen up to that point. Regardless, I dove headfirst into the fandom, and I've been a part of it ever since. One of the entries in a diary I kept when I was fourteen reads: "mam said *The X-Files* is just a TV show. What does she know?" I think for a lot of us, *The X-Files* is more than just a TV show. It's a cult hit that changed the way stories on television were told. It spawned a massive fandom that utilized the emerging technology of the internet. And it was able to capture the paranoia of the early nineties as well as reflect the changing times of the twenty-first century. Part history, part critical analysis, part love letter, this book attempts to capture all of that. I hope you will enjoy the chapters that follow, that they will make you think, reflect, and laugh, and that you'll forgive any mistakes.

Bethan Jones
January 2023

Introduction

"Why are people still watchin' a thirty-year-old TV show?"
- John Doggett ("Sunshine Days")

The question that opens this chapter is posed by Federal Bureau of Investigation Special Agent John Doggett in the season nine episode "Sunshine Days." In the episode, it's asked about *The Brady Bunch* as Doggett, Scully, and Reyes investigate a murder suspect obsessed with the show. But it's a question also relevant to *The X-Files*. Created by Chris Carter and premiering in 1993, the show ended in 2002 after declining viewing figures and a disappointing two seasons. While it was revived in 2016 following a long-running fan campaign, the success of the original nine seasons meant the show had become part of the cultural consciousness beyond the realm of fandom. It's rare that a TV show captures the public attention to this extent or is referred to in so many other pieces of media. Off the top of my head, I think of *Star Trek*, *Star Wars*, *The Simpsons*, and maybe *Friends* as other examples of film or TV—in the West at least—that are regularly quoted and recognized years after they first aired: say to someone "live long and prosper" or "I am your father" and they're likely to know where the reference is from[1]. "The Truth Is Out There" and "Trust No One"—two of *The X-Files*'s most iconic mottos—are regularly used

---

1   US audiences might have other shows to add to this list. I write this as a late Gen X/early millennial UK-based consumer of media.

in news articles and think pieces, and Mark Snow's distinctive theme tune, with its six-note whistle, has become a shortcut for highlighting the unexplained and weird (drawing yet another link between *The X-Files* and *The Twilight Zone*, whose four-note theme still evokes the uncanny and terrifying). During its original run, and for years afterward, *The X-Files* has been referenced in other media texts. Mulder and Scully appeared in the "Springfield Files" episode of *The Simpsons* in 1997 and were referenced in the 2005 pilot episode of *Bones* as well as in *Breaking Bad*, created by *X-Files* alumnus Vince Gilligan. More recently, its appearance in the 2022 episode of *Only Murders in the Building* "Flipping the Pieces" demonstrated the show's continuing relevance. But why *The X-Files* and not any of the other shows that debuted in 1993? I think there are a few reasons for this, including the connection between Mulder and Scully (played to critical acclaim by David Duchovny and Gillian Anderson), the dedicated fan base, and the show's ability to tap into the big questions of its time—perhaps more pertinent in 2016 than ever before.

When rumors began circulating about the possible return of *The X-Files*, the response from fans was, understandably, mixed. Some of these responses reflected on the final two seasons of the show and the disappointing 2008 film *I Want to Believe*; one fan, who responded to a questionnaire I posted online as part of my PhD research, wrote:

> Chris Carter has proven through the final season of the series, the series finale, and the 2008 movie, and his handling of the Mulder and Scully characters (and their relationship) that he is clearly unable to recapture what made *The X-Files* successful so many years ago. I don't hold out hope that Carter will be able to pull off anything that even comes close to what the series did and made me feel in the first 5 seasons.

Other responses, however, reflected on the ways in which politics, culture, and society had changed in the years since the show had ended and questioned whether *The X-Files* was still relevant. One fan wrote, "It was a good show that struck a cultural nerve when it came out. But that time has passed." In some ways, these fans were right.

The world in 2016 was radically different from the world in 2002: the US had seen a move from a Republican president to a Democrat—who also happened to be the first Black president; global migration had increased as a result of violence and political instability, seeing a corresponding increase in anti-immigrant rhetoric; and technology had advanced at a exponential rate. Also emerging in the 2000s and 2010s were a growing distrust of government and an evolution of conspiracy thinking. Some of the fans who responded to my survey questioned whether the show could really find a place in this new era, with one writing, "*The X-Files* was really a product of its time. After the second Iraq war and Dubya's bullshit and Edward Snowden's revelations, I don't think many people find gov't conspiracies and lies all that farfetched. I shrug at the mytharc these days. It's so . . . cute." And to some extent, who can blame them for that response? The idea that the US government was hiding the existence of extraterrestrial life from the population does seem rather naive when we consider the very real cover-ups that have been exposed over the last decade or so. Yet many others, explicitly referring to the paranoia, conspiracy theories, and politics of the original show, felt that those themes were perfect for the contemporary climate: an unsure time, politically, socially, economically, and technologically. Another fan wrote:

> Times have changed since the show went off the air in 2002—I'd like to see how Chris Carter and the other writers do a 21st century *X-Files* after all that has gone on with post 9/11 counterterrorism, Wikileaks and Edward Snowden, technology advances, social media, and more. What do people fear now? What is the tension between paranoia and skepticism in modern society? How much trust is there of government and other institutions?

These are all questions, I suggest over the course of this book, that *The X-Files* continues to address. While skepticism and distrust of the government certainly existed during the show's original run, fundamental changes within society meant that the revival seasons would need to deal with these in markedly different ways.

XXX

The first decade of the twenty-first century saw the financial crash of 2008, which led to increasing political instability, economic austerity, and a further polarization between left and the right across the globe—topics that seemed as pertinent to the show's concerns as the end of the Reagan presidency and the Cold War were to the original seasons (discussed in Chapter One). Although some viewers weren't sure if the revival would be able to adapt to a new landscape, many others (me included) felt that the themes the show originally dealt with were just as relevant. One fan wrote, "I think this is the perfect political climate for this revival to occur. The subject of the show is relevant now in ways that it might not necessarily have been since the release of *I Want to Believe*." Another felt that "now, in a time of government spying, and a new wave of disenchantment with the government and authority, the show is more relevant than ever." And these were ideas that Carter had actually been toying with for some time. In an interview with *The Guardian* newspaper, he highlighted the use of surveillance by the government as an influence for season ten, saying, "We're trying to be honest with the changes dealing with digital technology: the capability of spying. Clearly we're being spied on in the US—or at least spying on you—and there seems to be no shame in it."[2] He also noted the political changes and the way the show dealt with them in an interview with *Bustle*, saying:

> So much has changed politically since 1993, radical changes to 2001, radical changes through the Obama years, and even more radical change with President Trump. So *The X-Files* has gotten to deal with a lot of political realities, and I'll always think it's given the show a lot of its life. The political realities are part of the way we think about the show. But we're not responding to the political reality the way [shows like *American*

---

2   Dredge. 2015. "*X-Files* revival inspired by surveillance revelations, says show's creator." *The Guardian*.

Horror Story: Cult] are, where they're taking it head on.[3]

Those new political realities were referred to at various points throughout the season, though. In "This," Assistant Director Walter Skinner is refused assistance from the executive branch of the FBI because "the bureau's not in good standing with the White House"; in "Plus One," we see the (real world) conflict between a nameless president (Donald Trump) and the FBI, with Mulder telling Scully that the world is going to hell, with "the president working to bring down the FBI along with it." Perhaps most pertinently, though, we see the changing politics in the continued threat of a shadow government that poses a danger to democracy around the globe. The opening montage of "My Struggle III" includes footage of Trump's inauguration, Black Lives Matter protests, Vladimir Putin, and robed Ku Klux Klan members beneath a voice-over from Cigarette Smoking Man, who places himself at the center of the shadow government, "making sacrifices few are capable of, of which even fewer are willing," parceling out the truth, which is "held only by the few who know the levers of power." This statement draws parallels to the QAnon movement that emerged in late 2017 (discussed in Chapters Three and Six) and that argues that a secret cabal of Satan-worshiping child molesters poses a threat to global democracy. Donald Trump is the only person who could stop them, and the anonymous Q, who claims to be a high-ranking government official with access to classified information, parcels out snippets of information relating to this and encourages followers to reject any government officials other than Trump, the mainstream media, and medical experts.

QAnon developed from a conspiracy theory into a political movement, with followers appearing at Trump's reelection campaign rallies, Republican representatives failing to condemn—some even endorsing—the movement and its claims, and Trump and his allies attempting to overturn the results of the 2020 presidential election. This expansion of conspiracy theories into the mainstream seems a perfect

---

3   Thomas. 2018. "'*The X-Files*' Is Going To Give Donald Trump The Government Conspiracy Treatment." *Bustle.*

opportunity for a revival of *The X-Files*. Conspiracy theorists in the 1990s were like The Lone Gunmen: radical misfits, counterculturalists, and computer hackers who don't work but are financed by backers who believe in the cause. The Lone Gunmen, comprising Richard "Ringo" Langly, Melvin Frohike, and John Fitzgerald Byers, are on the fringes of society. They share a loft apartment that also functions as their office, rely on a 1974–79 VW Transporter to get around, and are often ridiculed for their beliefs—even Scully, after their first meeting, in "E.B.E.," tells Mulder, "Those were the most paranoid people I have ever met. I don't know how you could think that what they say is even remotely plausible." Fast-forward to the twenty-first century and conspiracy theorists are more akin to Tad O'Malley than Frohike, Langly, and Byers. When we first meet O'Malley, the host of a right-wing talk show in "My Struggle," he's in a black stretch limo, fully bulletproofed, with a bottle of Louis Montreuil champagne chilling on ice; later in the episode, he arrives at Mulder's house in a helicopter. As Mulder points out, conspiracy sells and has made O'Malley a very rich man. This mainstreaming of conspiracy is, perhaps, one of the biggest changes the show has had to contend with. Discussing season ten, Carter says he kept his finger to the wind and tried to figure out what was relevant and possible:

> People know the show deals with science and fact and also deals with far-flung theories about not only the supernatural but government conspiracies. It throws out as many questions as it does answers. And I have to say what [the conspiracy world has] done for me and the writers it has given us a whole new open field [in] which to run. It's given the show an interesting new life and context that it might not have had in 2002.[4]

This context deals not only with the mainstreaming of conspiracy theories but also the changing ways in which they circulate. The Lone Gunmen had an underground newsletter, called *The Magic Bullet*,

---

4   Hibberd. 2016. "Fox's 'X-Files' revival has controversial new theories." *Entertainment Weekly*.

circulated as hard copies to their subscribers; conspiracy theorists now have websites, Twitter accounts, Facebook pages, and YouTube channels through which they can spread their message.

This passage of time, and technology, is brought front and center in the revival seasons. In "My Struggle," O'Malley refers to "dirtboxes" recording conversations he would rather remain private—something Carter's production company, Ten Thirteen Productions, had to contend with in shooting the series: during one shoot, where they were filming green screen shots in a limousine, an aircraft was circling, which disrupted the shoot[5]—while in "The Lost Art of Forehead Sweat" online disinformation is highlighted as a major twenty-first century concern (discussed more in Chapter Six). Advances in technology were some of the key things fans mentioned in the questionnaire I circulated prior to season ten airing, with many excited about the possibilities new technology could bring to the storylines. In fact, technology was a staple throughout the revival seasons, and not just in relation to conspiracy theories: "Mulder and Scully Meet the Were-Monster" acknowledges the changing context most explicitly, riffing on the idea that those of an older generation struggle with new technology, with Mulder unable to make his new smartphone work and obtaining a grainy photograph of the monster's ear, or possibly its foot. "This" depicts some of the ethical quandaries of modern technology with Langly, whose consciousness is uploaded into a simulation that would come to life when he dies, warning Mulder and Scully that the virtual world is akin to an eternal prison with no escape; "Rm9sbG93ZXJz" warns about the dangers of artificial intelligence as Mulder and Scully eat at a fully automated restaurant before experiencing a range of increasingly dangerous interactions with artificially intelligent technology. The episode draws on the real-life example of a Microsoft chatbot designed to learn from human interactions that was shut down a day after it was released on Twitter because it had learnt to post racist and sexist messages. Carter and his coproducers made sure that *The X-Files* was able to tell stories that reflected the mid-2010s—

---

5   Tsukayama. 2016. "How technology changed 'The X-Files,' on-screen and off, according to its creator; Q&A." *The Independent*.

from conspiracy theories to the nature of truth to smartphones—and viewers responded positively: the first episode of season ten earned over 16 million viewers in the US based on live and same-day ratings, going up to 21.47 million when taking into account seven-day catch-up figures. Fox's assumption that reviving the series because it would be a ratings success seemed to have been proved right.

XXX

So why *are* we still watching a thirty-year old TV show? While I've talked about how seasons ten and eleven bring some of the themes of the earlier seasons up-to-date for a twenty-first century audience, what I haven't answered is *why* we're still watching. It is in part because Mulder and Scully are iconic leads who broke the mold and also because the stories themselves are compelling. But more than that, I think, the reason we keep coming back to the show is because of what it tells us about the time we're living in. *The X-Files* deals with the big questions: What is true? Whom can we trust? What kind of society do we want to live in? Is faith enough? And it does so in a way that speaks to the contemporary climate. When the series began, the effects of Watergate and Vietnam on the American population had been compounded by concerns about the approaching millennium and a move away from traditional religion; now the world is concerned with fake news and disinformation. The paranoia and distrust is still there, but it has a different cause. *The X-Files* highlights that, sometimes in ways that seem scarily prescient. As I watched the original series again while writing this book, the only thing that seemed dated was the technology (and yes, okay, Scully's pantssuits). Scully uses a desktop PC with a chunky CRT monitor to type up her fieldnotes; Mulder turns to a phone book to find Skyland Mountain rather than using Google Maps. Yet the cases they deal with, the questions they seek to answer, are ultimately timeless.

The rest of this book looks at some of the big issues *The X-Files* has dealt with over the course of its eleven seasons, as well as the way it has shaped the television landscape and the impact of the fandom. In writing this, I have attempted to speak to multiple readers, from the Philes, who watched the show when it first aired, to new fans who discovered the series on Netflix or via social media. To that end I've tried to combine broad-brush history with more detailed analyses covering all iterations of the show. For some readers, the impact of the Cold War on Carter or the influence Scully has had on generations of women may be old news, but for others—who perhaps aren't as familiar with the reams of articles and books written about the show—these insights might help give more context to the show and its enduring legacy. There are of course too many topics to address in one book, and you'll see references to other works that deal with some of these in more depth throughout the chapters. What I've done is divide the book into four sections that focus on the themes I think are most relevant, and I've structured these around the different eras of the show: the Vancouver years; the Los Angeles years; and the revival years. This isn't an arbitrary decision. The Vancouver years make excellent use of the locations in British Columbia to set the tone of the episodes and the overall series. It's dark, wooded, some might say gloomy (I'm not going to comment on the weather—when David Duchovny complained about the "four hundred inches of rainfall a day" in 1997, he incurred the wrath of thousands of the city's residents), and you can easily imagine some genetic throwback hiding in the trees. Cathy Johnson points out that the series has a 'signature style' that doesn't show the audience too much. John Bartley, director of photography on the first three seasons, described the show's style as "dark, moody, mysterious and sometimes claustrophobic[6]," and it's easy to see how Vancouver helped create this feel. Season five was originally planned to end the television series, the finale intended to transition the show into a film franchise. LA, where filming moved in 1998, ahead of season six, represented a new era for the series in terms of both storytelling and tone.

While season five ends in a typically dark, burned-out basement office, lit only by the flashing of emergency lights, season six opens

6   Johnson. 2005. "Quality/Cult Television: *The X-Files* and Television History." In Michael Hammond and Lucy Mazdon (eds) *The Contemporary Television Series*. Edinburgh University Press, p. 64.

with a blazing sun in a bright blue sky—a feature that becomes as much a part of the LA years as the Vancouver landscape did in the first five seasons. The lighting and landscape in "Drive," "The Rain King," and "Arcadia" is worlds away from those in episodes like the pilot, "War of the Coprophages," and "Detour," but the storytelling also changes. As Darren Mooney points out, "Triangle," the third episode of the season, "marked something of a shift [that] set the tone for the season[7]," which featured multiple quirky and comedic episodes hinting at a romantic relationship between Mulder and Scully. But just as the world inside the show was changing, so too was the world outside—with the millennium fast approaching, concerns abounded about a global computer malfunction, while the terrorist attacks of September 11, 2001, shook the country to its core and led to increasing faith in the government, although the anti-terrorism steps the Bush administration took to increasing suspicion in some circles. The ninth season was the last for the original iteration of the show; after 202 episodes and one movie, *The X-Files* appeared to be out of step with the mood of the country. Although the revival years technically begin with 2008's *I Want to Believe*, I mostly discuss seasons ten and eleven. A standalone monster-of-the-week narrative that didn't do that well in the box office (it would have been better suited for an autumn/winter release rather than the summer, when it had to compete with blockbusters like *The Dark Knight*), the film seemed unable to find a way to match the mood of the time—just like the final two seasons of the show years earlier. What really interests me in this era is how seasons ten and eleven tapped into the politics, fears, and paranoia of the 2010s. The show returned to Vancouver to film, giving us its original distinctive style, but updated to take into account smartphones, drones, and an increasing division between the ideals of left and right.

Section One, "Trust No One," focuses on politics, looking at conspiracy culture over the last three decades and the question of whom we can trust. Chapter One explores the initial impetus for the

---

7   Mooney. 2017. *Opening The X-Files: A Critical History of the Original Series*. McFarland, p. 112.

series—Watergate, the Cold War, and Vietnam—while Chapter Two examines the decline in viewers *The X-Files* encountered in its final four seasons and the effect that the change in attitudes toward the government following the September 11 attacks had on the show. Chapter Three brings us up to the revival years, in the context of Brexit, the Trump presidency, and the rise of QAnon.

Section Two, "The Truth Is Out There," takes a philosophical look at the series and what truth means in the context of *The X-Files*. The truth might be out there, but what exactly is it, how do we know it when we find it, and does it even matter anymore? Chapter Four analyzes "Jose Chung's 'From Outer Space'" and what the episode tells us about the nature of truth in both Klass 'County and in the wider show. Chapter Five examines faith and belief in the context of religion, especially in season seven, and asks whether the truth can be found not in science or doctrine but in other people. Chapter Six returns to a specific episode, this time analyzing the rise in fake news and disinformation following 9/11 and how that is addressed in the increasingly post-truth environment that "The Lost Art of Forehead Sweat" so satirically deals with.

Section Three, "I Want to Believe," examines the cultural contexts of *The X-Files* and some of the ways in which the show began to shape society as much as society shaped the show. Chapter Seven focuses on the way the show depicts gender and the subversion of gender expectations in the characters of Mulder and Scully, while Chapter Eight expands on this to examine how Scully inspired a generation of young girls to take up careers in science, technology, engineering, and medicine. Chapter Nine brings us up to the twenty-first century and how our understanding of gender and sexuality has changed, asking whether *The X-Files* changed along with it.

Section Four, "Deny Everything," takes us beyond the show itself to look at its impact on television, the growing franchise, and the show's fandom. Chapter Ten reflects on the impact *The X-Files* had on television more broadly, highlighting the producers and writers who have gone on to create some of the most acclaimed series in this latest "golden age" of TV. Chapter Eleven examines the franchise beyond the small screen. Fox, aware of the hit it had on its hands, expanded the story into spinoff shows, books, comics, and games, all of which allowed new entry points into *The X-Files* universe for new audiences and new ways for fans to engage with Mulder and Scully. Chapter Twelve turns to the fandom at-large, discussing the ways in which the history of the fandom is entwined with the history of the show itself and how fans of *The X-Files* have also had an impact on the real world. Finally, the conclusion reflects on some of the main themes and arguments made in the course of the book. It also asks what might happen now that Disney has acquired Fox and what the future might hold for *The X-Files*, a show with a history of transmedia storytelling and a large and dedicated fan base.

But first, let's go back to the beginning.

SECTION ONE

Trust No One

CHAPTER 1

Aliens, Watergate, and the Death of Trust

"What makes you think this is a conspiracy, that the government's involved?"
- Scully ("Memento Mori")

The X-Files is built on conspiracies. While the show's most famous motto might be "The Truth Is Out There," its underlying principle is to trust no one. We see this in the very first episode—in his efforts to find out what really happened to his sister, Samantha, Mulder discovers the existence of a global conspiracy to colonize Earth. Scully is sent to debunk Mulder's ideas and discredit him given the risks he poses to the project. In one of the most iconic scenes of the series, we see Scully enter the X-Files's basement home and approach Mulder, where the following exchange takes place:

> SCULLY: Agent Mulder. I'm Dana Scully, I've been assigned to work with you.
> MULDER: Oh, isn't it nice to be suddenly so highly regarded? So, who did you tick off to get stuck with this detail, Scully?

> SCULLY: Actually, I'm looking forward to working with
> you. I've heard a lot about you.
> MULDER: Oh, really? I was under the impression that
> you were sent to spy on me.

Scully immediately offers her qualifications, but these aren't what will make Mulder trust her—they're not always necessary in this line of work. *The X-Files*'s focus on aliens and the paranormal is a large part of the show's success and a testament to Carter's understanding of the cultural moment at the time. David Lavery, Angela Hague, and Maria Cartwright, editors of one of the first academic books on the show, point out that the American public's interest with UFOs, which began with the Roswell incident in 1947, transformed into a fascination with abduction that linked *The X-Files* to a larger cultural and historical context. B movies like *Invasion of the Body Snatchers* (1956) and *The Thing from Another World* (1951) had introduced audiences to the idea of alien invasion, while books such as John Fuller's *The Interrupted Journey* (1966) and Whitley Strieber's *Communion* (1987) had suggested a more personal and invasive encounter. *The X-Files* took this one step farther, combining "the most terrifying aspects of paranormal experience with various cultural elements: science fiction; New Age obsessions with channeling, reincarnation, near-death experiences, and spiritual advancement; Byzantine government conspiracy stories, which include secret medical experiments upon unsuspecting citizens; and concerns with sexual abuse and genetic engineering"[1]. An increase in tabloid stories, TV shows and magazines dedicated to the paranormal seemed to spring up in the late 1980s and 1990s. Certainly I was interested in the paranormal before I began watching the show. One of the books I remember as a kid was about unexplained phenomena like the Loch Ness Monster and extrasensory perception, and I was fascinated by those topics. The paranormal and the supernatural seemed to proliferate on television during the eighties and nineties. Although science fiction series like *Star Trek*, *Doctor Who*,

---

1   Lavery, Hague, and Cartwright. 1996. "Introduction: Generation X—*The X-Files* and the Cultural Moment." In David Lavery, Angela Hague, and Marla Cartwright (eds) *Deny All Knowledge: Reading The X-Files*. Faber and Faber, p. 7.

and *The Six Million Dollar Man* had been relatively popular since the 1960s these offered a more optimistic approach to the genre than the more ominous series that followed, such as *The Invaders*, a paranoid show about alien invasion that aired for two seasons in the late sixties and whose lead actor, Roy Thinnes, played alien rebel Jeremiah Smith in *The X-Files*. Aaron John Gulyas, in his book *The Paranormal and the Paranoid*, points out that *The X-Files* didn't emerge in a vacuum, highlighting the history of alien-contact science fiction television and films that became popular in the 1950s. The series further adopted elements of the paranormal, extraterrestrial, and conspiratorial culture that had developed in the 1970s. Shows like *Kolchak: The Night Stalker* and *Project U.F.O.* used specific paranormal incidents as inspiration for episodes, while films including *The Conversation* (1974), *The Parallax View* (1974), *Three Days of the Condor* (1975), and *All the President's Men* (1976) brought paranoia and conspiracy onto the big screen. Documentary series like *In Search Of . . .*, which began as three hour-long specials, including one inspired by Erich von Däniken's 1968 book *Chariots of the Gods? Unsolved Mysteries of the Past*, "presented casual television viewers with a wide variety of supernatural and conspiratorial topics ranging from alien abductions to the Loch Ness Monster"[2] while also familiarizing viewers "with the allegedly factual basis of many of the foundational stories and myths of the paranormal, especially those connected with UFOs and belief in alien visitation and abduction."[3] Figures like Whitley Strieber, whose book about his abduction experiences was published in 1987; Uri Geller, who became famous for his apparent psychokinetic powers and telepathy; and David Icke, a British conspiracy theorist who claimed that an interdimensional race of reptilian beings had hijacked Earth, were also featured prominently on television in the 1990s, further mainstreaming various conspiracy and paranormal theories. But if the focus on the paranormal was indicative of the cultural moment of the

---

2   Gulyas. 2015. *The Paranormal and the Paranoid: Conspiratorial Science Fiction Television.* Rowman & Littlefield, p. 26.

3   Ibid.

THE TRUTH IS STILL OUT THERE

early 1990s, its underlying themes of distrust and paranoia dated back to earlier cultural events in the US.

XXX

One of the key inspirations for the show, and an event that had a huge impact on Carter himself, was the Watergate scandal. The arrest of several burglars who had broken into the Democratic National Committee office in the Watergate building led to the resignation of President Richard Nixon when it was revealed that the burglars were linked to his reelection committee and he had not only taken steps to cover up the crime but also swore to the public that none of his staff had been involved. Nixon was reelected in a landslide victory after making that speech, but the fact that he had lied to the electorate resulted in many Americans losing faith in their government. Talking to the New York *Daily News*, Carter said, "I was about 15 or 16 years old when Watergate happened and I think that ruined me forever as far as my belief in institutions and in authority and agendas of government."[4] Despite the fact it took place twenty years before the pilot of *The X-Files* episode aired, Watergate reverberated through the first nine seasons of the show. Mulder's first informant, Deep Throat, was inspired by the real-life Deep Throat, who leaked information on the Watergate scandal to *Washington Post* reporter Bob Woodward (and who was finally revealed, in 2005, to be Mark Felt, an assistant FBI associate director at the time). Although Deep Throat's run on the series was short-lived (he was killed in the season one finale, "The Erlenmeyer Flask"), the character set the tone for the conspiratorial nature of the series. Brian Lowry, in the first official episode guide, noted he "helped establish a tone and undercurrent of gravity on *The X-Files* that was to provide the spine of the series."[5] What Deep Throat also did was connect *The X-Files* to a time that had shaken Americans

---

4   Beale and Caruso. 1998. "'X' Drive Chris Carter Brings His *X-Files* Passions And Obsessions To The Big Screen." *Daily News*.

5   Lowry. 1995. *The Truth Is Out There: The Official Guide To The X-Files*. Harper Collins, p. 91.

to the core and underscored the idea that the government could not be trusted. Despite acting as an informant to Mulder, he has his own secrets to keep, as we see in a flashback during "Musings of a Cigarette Smoking Man," in which he kills an alien. Deep Throat is part of the syndicate responsible for working with the aliens to colonize Earth, a shadowy organization within the government that for Rob Bowman, one of the show's directors, represents "betrayal from the Watergate days. They wield power without conscience."[6]

Watergate was a recurring motif throughout the series—in season one's "E.B.E.," Mulder refers to Watergate alongside a series of other conspiracies or government cover-ups: John F. Kennedy's assassination, radiation experiments on terminal patients, Iran-Contra, and Roswell. In season two's "Little Green Men," we see a flashback to the night of Samantha's abduction with a television news report about Watergate playing in the background; in the same episode, Mulder stays at the Watergate Hotel. In season six's "One Son," Mulder visits Cigarette Smoking Man at the Watergate Apartments in the hope of discovering the truth about his sister's disappearance. Watergate was important because it showed that the American government was willing to lie to its people to preserve power at any cost, and if it could lie about domestic espionage, it could also lie about the existence of extraterrestrials. In fact, we see a cover-up in the second episode of the show, aptly titled "Deep Throat," when US Air Force pilots begin behaving erratically after testing experimental aircraft. Mulder breaks into the base and witnesses a triangular-shaped craft hovering above him before he's captured by military officers who then wipe his memory, leaving him unable to remember how he got there or what he saw. One of the suggestions this episode makes is summed up by security officer Paul Mossinger, who tells Mulder, "Everything you've seen here is equal to the protection we give it. It's you who have acted inappropriately." This warning that some things should be hidden from the general public is something many governments seem to have taken to heart.

But while Watergate was an important turning point, it wasn't

6   Hurwitz and Knowles. 2008. *The Complete X-Files*. Insight Editions, p. 75.

THE TRUTH IS STILL OUT THERE

the only influence on the show; the Cold War also looms large over *The X-Files*. The Cold War began shortly after the end of the Second World War, which is another recurring theme in the show, as we discover that the US government is involved in a vast conspiracy to perform experiments on American citizens, working with former Nazi and Japanese scientists and aliens. Paranoid about the threat of communism, the US government began spying on its own people. J. Edgar Hoover, head of the FBI at the time, authorized the agency to surveil, wiretap, and infiltrate groups that he thought posed a threat, and this is echoed in the show when Mulder's and Scully's phones are being wiretapped on multiple occasions and when Mulder is assigned to wiretap duty in "Little Green Men." The impact of the Cold War on Carter, and its relevance to Mulder's work on the X-Files, is made most evident in season five's "Travelers," in which Mulder investigates the death of Edward Skur, a man he believes may have had some connection to his father. Mulder seeks out retired FBI Arthur Dales, and in a flashback to 1952, we discover Dales was encouraged by J. Edgar Hoover himself to track down Skur, who was suspected of being a Communist. In the episode we discover that Skur is actually wanted by the authorities because he was experimented on and is seeking revenge, but disguising this beneath the threat of communism allows the episode to function on two levels. First, it is a reflection on the nature of the series itself. As Robert Shearman points out in his review, it "juxtaposes the ideas of 'serving' as being a patriot, with 'resisting' as being branded a traitor"[7] and asks us to consider Mulder's position in relation to each. Mulder had previously made a name for himself as the best analyst in the Violent Crimes Unit, yet on beginning work on the X-Files, he is moved to a basement office, he and his work considered a threat. Mulder is essentially blacklisted despite his obvious skill as an investigator, which I think we can see as reminiscent of the blacklisting that took place under US Senator Joseph McCarthy in the 1940s and 50s. And this is where the episode functions on a second, real-world, level. In 1947,

---

7   Shearman. 2009. *Wanting to Believe: A Critical Guide to The X-Files, Millennium & The Lone Gunmen*. Mad Norwegian Press, pp. 138-139.

near the beginning of the Cold War, nine days of hearings were held into the Communist Party's influence in Hollywood. In total, over three hundred industry professionals were boycotted by the studios, including Charlie Chaplin, Orson Welles, and—as A. J. Black points out in his article for The Companion—Howard Dimsdale, who had taught screenwriting to the episode's writers, John Shiban and Frank Spotnitz, at the American Film Institute.[8] The episode serves as a tribute to Dimsdale, who had worked for several years in Europe after being blacklisted and secretly wrote Hollywood movies under the pen name Arthur Dales.

While much is made of the impact that Watergate and the Cold War had on *The X-Files*, academic Charles Taylor argues that it is almost impossible to understand *The X-Files* without taking into account the wider political, cultural, and economic context of its time, writing that "what links up the show to the zeitgeist is that Mulder and Scully are working to get out from under the most enduring legacy of the Regan/Bush era: the way government proclaims [. . .] that the truth is irrelevant."[9] Bill Clinton became president in 1993, marking the end of more than a decade of Republican leadership during which an actor and a businessman had piloted the course of the country, and there were growing economic and cultural divisions within society. The end of the Cold War at the beginning of the 1990s also saw America looking not outward toward an enemy, but inward, and fears about immigration, globalization, national identity, and technology emerged. M. A. Crang in his book *Denying the Truth: Revisiting The X-Files after 9/11* suggests that the show's emergence during the Clinton era can be seen "as a response to the *beginning* of a world no longer characterized by the same political certainties."[10] As Carter noted in a 1994 interview, "Now that Russia is no longer our very recognizable enemy, we suddenly need to find other enemies and other sources of

8   Dimsdale was a screenwriter who wrote under the name Arthur Dales, the name given to a recurring character in the show.

9   Taylor. 1994. "Truth Decay: Sleuths after Reagan." *Millennium Pop* 1.1.

10   Crang. 2015. *Denying the Truth: Revisiting The X-Files after 9/11*. CreateSpace Independent Publishing Platform, p. 11.

discontent."[11] One of those enemies became the US government.

XXX

While the shadow of Watergate hangs over *The X-Files*, the US was also grappling with political shifts during the 1990s that came with their own machinations and lies. Scholar Elyce Rae Helford describes the Clinton years as "sameness reconstructed to appear as progressive shift,"[12] and despite his campaign commitments to topics like universal healthcare and gay rights, Clinton became embroiled in scandals just as his Republican predecessors had. Allegations were made of criminal conduct relating to the Whitewater Development Corporation land deal while Clinton was still governor of Arkansas, and he was accused of multiple counts of sexual harassment, including rape, eventually admitting to two affairs, including one with White House intern Monica Lewinksy that eventually led to his 1998 impeachment. Clinton was also linked to a number of conspiracy theories; the *Washington Post* claimed that his first term "marked the dawn of a new age of conspiracy theory."[13] Among the theories put forth was the Clinton Body count, which became popular following the death of Deputy White House counsel Vince Foster. Although Foster's death was ruled a suicide, right-wing agitators circulated the theory that it (and several other deaths) was actually a murder ordered by Clinton to silence his political opponents.

Douglas Kellner argues that *The X-Files* instilled "distrust toward established authority, representing institutions of government and the established order as highly flawed, even complicit in the worst crimes and evil imaginable,"[14] though I'd say it was less that the show instilled

---

11 Maccarillo. 1994. "A Conversation with *The X-Files* creator Chris Carter." *SciFi Entertainment*.

12 Helford. 2000. *Fantasy Girls: Gender in the New Universe of Science Fiction and Fantasy Television*. Rowman & Littlefield, p. 6.

13 Thomas. 1994. "Clinton Era Conspiracies! Was Gennifer Flowers on the Grassy Knoll? Probably Not, but Here Are Some Other Bizarre Theories for a New Political Age." *The Washington Post*.

14 Kellner. 1999. "*The X-Files* and the aesthetics and politics of postmodern pop." *Journal of Aesthetics and Art Criticism* 57 (2), p. 169.

distrust and more that it leveraged the growing number of reports about the government's secretive activities to inspire its storylines. In the wake of the siege of the Branch Davidians compound in Waco, Texas, in 1993, right-wing conspiracy groups argued that the danger was caused by the government itself in an attempt to curtail liberties, while those on the left felt that collusion between the government and corporations, as already evidenced by scandals under Reagan and Bush, was the real issue. We see both of these emerging in the monster-of-the-week stories in the first few seasons of the show. Season four's "The Field Where I Died" not only refers to the siege at David Koresh's Waco compound but almost foretells the Heaven's Gate mass suicides that took place in San Diego the following year. In the episode, the FBI and the Bureau of Alcohol, Tobacco, and Firearms raid a compound belonging to a local fundamentalist cult called the Temple of the Seven Stars. Although the compound is empty, cult leader Vernon Ephesian and his six wives are discovered in an underground bunker about to commit mass suicide by drinking poisoned juice (in reference to the Jonestown massacre in 1978, when members of the Peoples Temple committed suicide by drinking poisoned Flavor Aid). The episode takes place just three years after the siege at the Branch Davidians compound, at a time when the context (if not its theme of past lives) was still front and center in the minds of many Americans.

By February 1993, the Branch Davidians were preparing for an apocalypse that leader David Koresh predicted would take place in Texas. Their plan, according to former member David Bunds, was to hole up at Mount Carmel and await the moment when the American Army attacked and brought about the end of the world.[15] The group had stockpiled food, water, firearms, and gas masks, so was prepared when the ATF attempted to execute a search warrant relating to the alleged possession of a possibly illegal arms cache on the site. Although reports are conflicted on who opened fire first, the initial raid resulted in a gunfight between the compound and the ATF that killed five agents and five Branch Davidians. What followed was a fifty-one-day

15   Kantrowitz. 1993. "The Messiah Of Waco." *Newsweek*.

siege in which the FBI, which had taken over from the ATF, attempted to breach the compound, culminating in the government using armored vehicles to insert CS gas into the wooden building in which every member of the Branch Davidians had barricaded themselves. The building was subsequently set alight on Koresh's orders. Almost all of the members of the cult died in the siege, along with four law enforcement officers. Glen Morgan and James Wong, who wrote the episode, draw overt parallels to both Koresh and Jim Jones, leader of the Peoples Temple. "I don't care if you think that I'm Jim Jones or David Koresh," Ephesian tells the agents. "I don't need you to believe or even like me." Mulder and Scully's boss, FBI Assistant Director Walter Skinner, tells Scully he's concerned that a "federal investigation will ignite Ephesian's paranoia to such a degree that we won't have another Waco on our hands; we'll have Jonestown"—a prophetic response, since the episode's ending mirrors both the Jonestown massacre and the siege of Waco. As ATF agents close in on the Temple of the Seven Stars, cult members begin firing on them. Inside, Ephesian preaches to his followers, who drink poisoned juice.

Responding to Waco, President Clinton denied the FBI bore any responsibility for the deaths, saying, "I do not think the United States government is responsible for the fact that a bunch of religious fanatics decided to kill themselves."[16] While many Americans also felt that the Branch Davidians got what they deserved, the incident nevertheless proved a rallying point for the far right, which felt that the US government not only had overreached, but had become a threat to freedom itself. As former FBI profiler Clint Van Zandt recalls, "I can still remember a bumper sticker I saw on a pickup truck shortly after the destruction at Waco. It said, 'I love my country, it's the government I'm afraid of.'"[17] The government had indeed become an enemy now that the Soviet threat of the Cold War was over, and Waco played a key role. As A. J. Black points out in his article "The Field Where I Died," many people believe that Waco was, during the

16 Burton. 2018. "The Waco tragedy, explained." *Vox.*

17 Van Zandt. 2008. "Remembering Waco and Okla. City bombing." *NBC News.*

early 1990s, "a formative inspiration for not just Timothy McVeigh's Oklahoma City bombing (which would influence the opening of the first *X-Files* movie), but also the ongoing rise and proliferation of right-wing American militia movements."[18] We see this theme revisited in season five's "The Pine Bluff Variant," in which Mulder attempts to infiltrate a domestic terrorist organization called the New Spartans who have "the expressed goal of overthrowing the federal government." Interestingly, the virus introduced in season ten is called the Spartan Virus. Coincidence?

<u>**XXX**</u>

The increasing surveillance of, and interference in, the life of the American public is a recurring undercurrent in the series, as I mentioned earlier, and this ties in to larger questions about technology that *The X-Files* is concerned with. As scholar Kevin Howley writes, the show "is an expression of deep-seated cultural anxieties toward various forms of control technologies."[19] Scientific discoveries often go hand in hand with technological advances, and advances in technology can also be used to control people. We see this in episodes like "Wetwired," where a device attached to a telephone pole emits signals that tap into people's paranoid delusions and lead them to kill, and "SR 819," in which Skinner's circulatory system fails because he has been infected with nanotechnology controlled by a remote device in the hands of a shadow government that wants to limit Mulder and Scully's access to the X-Files. These concerns clearly mirror those of the general population, which had become aware of government agencies using technology to both spy on and influence the public.

The show also deals with another question that has concerned science fiction writers for decades—artificial intelligence. We see this as early as "Ghost in the Machine," the seventh episode of season one. In the episode, Mulder and Scully investigate the death of Benjamin

---

18   Black. 2022. "*The X-Files*|'The Field Where I Died' and Charismatic Cult Leaders." *The Companion.*

19   Howley. 2001. "Spooks, Spies, and Control Technologies in *The X-Files*." *Television & New Media*, 2(3), p. 258.

Drake, CEO of a technology company. Although the company's founder, Brad Wilczek, is suspected of the murder—the two had argued about downsizing before Drake was killed—the company's central operating system is actually responsible. We discover that the COS is a form of artificial intelligence designed by Wilczek and wanted by the Department of Defense. As the episode progresses, Mulder and Scully discover how intelligent the COS is—it hacks into Scully's home computer, cuts the power to the building as the agents make their way inside to investigate, and nearly kills Scully by pulling her into a giant fan when she climbs into an air vent. While "Ghost in the Machine" clearly pays homage to Stanley Kubrick's *2001: A Space Odyssey*, the episode also asks questions about free will and what intelligence actually is. While the technology might seem dated now (and episode writers Howard Gordon and Alex Gansa admit they weren't computer literate, which they felt was a detriment to the episode), the questions are still pertinent, especially as artificial intelligence develops more and more applications. The way that Carter and his writers deal with what technology could do and the implications of that are scarily prophetic. And it's not just technology in the physical world that the show deals with—it's also humans in the virtual world. The internet was taking off just as *The X-Files* aired, and the show was a popular topic of conversation online. The internet as a form of communication technology was also a force to be distrusted. In season five's "Kill Switch," written by cyberpunk authors William Gibson and Tom Maddox, Mulder and Scully deal with an artificial intelligence that has been 'let loose' on the internet. Whereas Brad Wilczek was depicted as a counterculture hippy in "Ghost in the Machine" (he spent a year following around the Grateful Dead before starting his company in his parents' garage), Donald Gelman in "Kill Switch" is "a Silicon Valley folk hero" whom Lone Gunman Byers describes as "a visionary, not a capitalist. A subversive." Gelman created a sentient artificial intelligence program that he then released online to see if it would evolve in its natural environment. The program, much like the earlier COS, evolves too well and resorts to violence at any attempt to destroy it.

The era surrounding *The X-Files*'s original series was in some ways an odd one. Technology was advancing at a blinding pace, and with that came concerns about how it would be used and what implications it had for humanity. "Kill Switch" seems to "present the internet as a place of almost limitless potential," as the Movie Blog review of the episode suggests.[20] In a discussion with Scully, Esther, Gelman's colleague, describes how she and her lover planned to "enter the AI, give up our inefficient bodies so that our consciousness could live together forever," seeing the internet as a place of endless opportunity, yet season three's "2Shy" positions the internet as a dangerous place: Virgil Encanto uses online chatrooms to find lonely women whom he seduces and ultimately kills. As one fan told me, the original series existed in "that rare era both pre- and post- technology takeover," and many of the episodes as well as the show's underlying themes attempt to grapple with that double-edged sword.

---

20   The M0vie Blog. 2015. "*The X-Files*–Kill Switch (Review).

CHAPTER 2

The Swift Decline of Subversive Television

"What's really on trial here is the truth."
– Mulder ("The Truth")

Carter had originally intended for *The X-Files* to transition into a film franchise at the end of season five, but the success of the first five seasons of the show meant that Fox was loath to let go of a show that was so lucrative, so two additional seasons were ordered. This meant that the season six opener, "The End," had to segue from both the season five finale and *Fight the Future*, which had been intended as the first installment of the film franchise. Although the episode performed well, fans and critics were divided. The move to LA undoubtedly shifted the tone of the series, and most of the crew members working on the show were new. Season six was not only visually lighter (as showcased in Vince Gilligan's "Drive," which sees Mulder driving from Nevada into California), but also featured an increase in the number of tonally lighter, comedic monster-of-the-week episodes. In the well-received "Triangle" for example, Mulder finds himself onboard a British passenger liner that has appeared in the Bermuda Triangle. The ship and its passengers appear to be stuck in 1939 along with German soldiers who are searching for a weapon that could grant them victory in the forthcoming war. The series's regular characters are reimagined as German soldiers, and the style of filming and editing is modeled on Alfred Hitchcock's *Rope*. At the end of the episode, a delirious Mulder tells Scully he loves her ("Oh, brother" is her response). "Triangle" was followed by "Dreamland," which features a memorable scene in which David Duchovny and Michael McKean perform the dance from the 1933 Marx Brothers comedy *Duck Soup*, and other lighter episodes during the season included "How the Ghosts Stole Christmas," "Arcadia," and "The Unnatural"

For some fans, this marked the decline of the show. The stand-alone episodes weren't scary enough and focused too much on horror or romance. The move away from the overarching conspiracy theory also angered some viewers, as Jo-Ann Parks noted in Space.com: "There are even those who simply think the show has too many stand-alone episodes. These fans find the sudden shifts between Mulder and Scully almost uncovering the great government-consortium-alien conspiracy and then chasing after random monsters distressing."[1] The nature of the conspiracy changed dramatically in season six, however, with the destruction of the Syndicate at the hands of alien rebels in the two-part "Two Fathers"/"One Son." Frank Spotnitz explained this, saying, "Our feeling was that the mythology was becoming an awful lot for people to continue to keep track of"[2]—a fair assessment according to fans and critics who were becoming increasingly fed up with the convoluted mytharc. Carter has reflected on the changes in season six, saying that it's possible to see *The X-Files* in two parts: "You can look at the show as pre-'Two Fathers'/'One Son' and post 'Two Fathers'/'One Son.'"[3] Indeed, when the mytharc finally returned at the end of season

---

1   Parks. 2000. "What's Ailing *The X-Files*?" Space.com.

2   Perenson. 1999. "Executive producer Frank Spotnitz looks to the future of *The X-Files*." *SciFi Entertainment*.

3   Lee. 1999. "'The X-Files': Burning Question." *Entertainment Weekly*.

six, it tied the alien mythology of the early seasons in with human creation and seemed to suggest that the origin of human life was extraterrestrial.

Carter and Spotnitz were influenced by ancient astronaut theory, popularized by Erich von Däniken, who suggested that the gods and angels depicted in ancient art and mythologies were intelligent aliens who had visited earth and made contact with humans. Von Däniken hypothesized that ancient structures, like the Pyramids in Egypt and the Nazca Lines in Peru, reflect more sophisticated knowledge than existed when they were created and must have been influenced by alien visitors or 'ancient astronauts' - an idea clearly expressed in "Biogenesis." This exploration of the origin of human life continued into season seven and foregrounded religion in the new mythology, not only suggesting that aliens had developed the notions of God and religion but also drawing parallels between Mulder and Christ (which I talk about more in Chapter Five). In an interview with *Entertainment Weekly*, Spotnitz explained this was a deliberate ploy: "It's a conjunction of science and mysticism, of aliens and religion, that we're starting to develop. It's deliberate on our part, to help bring all the mythologies together into one storyline."[4] This attempt wasn't entirely successful. Although the ancient alien theory was returned to in season nine's "Provenance" and "Providence"—this time in relation to Mulder and Scully's son, William—many fans and critics felt the show was running out of steam. Critic Darren Mooney suggests that season six marked a turning point for both the show's viewing figures and cultural cache.

The series lost almost a quarter of its audience over the course of season six, which also marked the first time since *The X-Files* had premiered that it wasn't nominated for Outstanding Drama Series at the Emmy Awards. The show's ratings continued to decline over the following three seasons, not helped by Duchovny leaving the series at the end of season seven. The show introduced two new characters in season eight, John Doggett and Monica Reyes, who aided Scully in

4   Hurwitz and Knowles. 2008, p.159.

her search for Mulder, but for fans and critics, the show just wasn't the same. As one fan said, "Season seven feels different—as if the production team was running out of steam and ended up making more of an *X-Files* rip-off/parody than actual *X-Files*. As for seasons 8 and 9, I do my best to forget they ever happened. To me, *X-Files* is Mulder and Scully, and neither of them are replaceable." Although the show was losing viewers, it still drew audiences of well over ten million during seasons seven and eight. The political and cultural climate was to change dramatically a few months before season nine aired, however, sealing the show's fate.

XXX

On the morning of September 11, 2001, two planes crashed into the north and south Towers of the World Trade Center, with a third crashing into the Pentagon. The attacks killed 2,977 people from ninety-three nations, including forty people who died while preventing Flight 93 from crashing into the Capitol building in Washington D.C. Planned and executed by Al-Qaeda, an Islamic terrorist organization, the attacks were designed to strike targets deemed symbolic of American power. The events of that day had an immediate impact on television. As Paul A. Cantor points out:

> In the first few days following, broadcasting schedules had to be hastily reshuffled. For example, the Fox Network canceled a showing of the movie *Independence Day* advertised for September 15. The movie's trademark shot of the White House exploding was exactly what Americans did not want to see so soon after witnessing all-too-similar disasters in the real world. Late-night talk-show hosts such as David Letterman and Jay Leno were open about their reluctance to go ahead with their normal comedy routines at a time when the nation was more inclined to grieve than to laugh.[5]

---

5   Cantor. 2012. *The Invisible Hand in Popular Culture: Liberty Vs. Authority in American Film and TV.* The University Press of Kentucky, p. 278.

HBO suspended promotion for the second episode of *Band of Brothers*, and production on *The X-Files* stopped for the day despite filming taking place in LA. Robert Patrick recalls filming "Daemonicus" the day after the attacks: "It was the first time that I couldn't do my lines. I really took a lot of pride in showing up prepared. And I just couldn't do it. The dialogue was all about demonic possession, and it just was freaking me out."[6] After the attack, George W. Bush, who had become president after Bill Clinton in January 2001, addressed the nation, stating his intention to wage war on terror, beginning with Al-Qaeda. The American people rallied together behind Bush, and public expressions of patriotism, like displaying the American flag, surged. Almost overnight, it seemed the world of *The X-Files* was no longer reflective of the one Americans lived in. One of the story arcs of season eight involved the US government genetically engineering "super soldiers" by experimenting on citizens, which seemed out of touch with the mood of the post-9/11 US. In fact, Fox delayed the season nine premiere, part one of the two-part "Nothing Important Happened Today," by a few weeks before finally airing it on November 11, 2001.

The X-Files had long been considered a subversive show, suggesting if not implicitly encouraging viewers to distrust authority and the government. In fact, one of Carter's intentions with the show was to "jolt people out of their complacency" by showing them "that in the absence of political or public mindedness, the people who wield the power will wield it in dangerous ways."[7] The Syndicate certainly showed us that, reaching into every arm of the federal government as well as—potentially—governments overseas (the Syndicate met in London in *Fight the Future*). Scholars Enrica Picarelli and M. Carmen Gomez-Galisteo argue that the show could get away with questioning the US government because it was broadcast at a time when the US seemed safe from international terrorism—though domestic terrorism was an issue, as discussed in the last chapter—with the end of the

6   Hurwitz and Knowles 2008, p. 200.

7   Goldman. 1996. *The X-Files Book of the Unexplained, Volume II*. Harper Prism, p. 25.

Cold War, threats from overseas weren't considered as seriously. When 9/11 happened, it "demanded a strong government to protect citizens and restore their trust in their very safety—notions at odds with the distrust *The X-Files* promoted."[8] This distrust of the government was evident in season nine as the super soldiers plotline advanced, but as episodes continued to be produced, the writers had to balance the mytharc and the storylines that had started seasons earlier with the changed mood in the country. Talking to *TV Guide*, Spotnitz said 9/11 wasn't going to affect what the writers did in a literal way, but it couldn't help but affect the stories they were telling:

> We're working on a mythology [episode] now and you want to find a way to be thematically relevant and say something true about fighting evil and fanaticism and irrationality. But you want to do it in a way that is appropriate and doesn't trivialize what's really going on in the world. We've got a certain palette to paint on, which is the paranormal, and it just does not feel at all appropriate to mix that with real-life events.[9]

While the show's earlier seasons had touched a chord with audiences, the events of 9/11 understandably turned viewers' attention away from the skies and across the seas. With a war on terror declared and the American government enjoying widespread support the show's focus on super soldiers and the colonization of Earth by aliens seemed remote from the daily fears of living in a post-9/11 world. The government spying on its citizens, a syndicate masterminding an alien takeover of Earth, experiments being carried out on an unwilling public—none of these were what audiences wanted in the wake of an attack on their way of life. It's perhaps no surprise that *The X-Files*'s ratings continued falling after the season nine finale. Meanwhile, a new Fox series, 24, had premiered on November 6, 2001, following counterterrorism

---

8   Picarelli and Gomez-Galisteo. 2013. "Be fearful: *The X-Files'* post-9/11 legacy." *Science Fiction Film and Television*, 6(1), p. 82.

9   Ausiello. 2001a. "*X-Files* Reacts to 9-11." *TV Guide*.

agent Jack Bauer as he protected Senator David Palmer from an assassination plot on the day of the California presidential primary. The difference between the two series couldn't be more stark. While both Mulder, prior to his disappearance in season eight, and Bauer are working for the government, Mulder is trying to bring it down from within while Bauer is protecting it from outside forces. Bauer was a patriot; Mulder and Scully were all too aware of the shortcomings of the US. Darren Mooney points out that although *24* went into production before 9/11, it "consciously spoke to the nation's anxieties and uncertainties"[10] and did so in a way *The X-Files* could not.

XXX

While it's understandable that *The X-Files*'s ratings fell in the immediate aftermath of 9/11, it is somewhat surprising that the mood of the United States seemed so out of step with the show. Enrica Picarelli and M. Carmen Gomez-Galisteo suggest that 9/11 sounded the death knell for the series because "in the aftermath of 9/11, the 'Trust No One' of *The X-Files* became too subversive and out of touch with the public need to trust the government to keep it safe from future attacks."[11] Yet one of the ways in which the government intended to keep people safe involved increased surveillance—something the show had warned about on numerous occasions. The Patriot Act expanded the surveillance abilities of law enforcement to allow for the tapping of domestic and international phones; authorized the indefinite detention without trial of immigrants; and gave law enforcement permission to search property and records without a warrant or even the knowledge of the owner. Episode six of season nine, "Trust No 1," is an almost Orwellian tale about surveillance that takes up these themes. The tagline was changed for this episode from "The Truth Is Out There" to "They're Watching," and the teaser sequence features stills from past episodes edited to look as though they're taken from

---

10   Mooney 2017, p. 163.

11   Picarelli and Gomez-Galisteo 2013, p. 83.

surveillance cameras. The Patriot Act was signed into law on October 26, 2001, following not only 9/11 but also the anthrax attacks that had begun on September 18 and lasted for several weeks. Paul A. Cantor, reflecting on the scenes of personnel in hazmat suits decontaminating buildings, writes that "the real world seemed to have been plunged into an *X-Files* episode. I remember thinking at the time not how outdated the series was, but how prophetic it had turned out to be."[12] This may be one reason why the show's ratings fell. People wanted either comfort (in the form of shows like *24*, which showed the US protecting its citizens from outside threats) or escapism. *The X-Files*, its original conceit of aliens and UFOs inextricably tied in with a corrupt shadow government attacking the very heart of democracy, was neither of these. The show's focus on aliens also seemed both relevant to, and dangerous in, a post-9/11 world. Aliens on the show stood in for illegal immigrants, who had been perceived by some as a constant threat to not just the US but other first world nations throughout the series's run. The introduction of super soldiers in season eight mirrors this escalating concern, as the government works against the aliens in order to save Earth in a way that could be read as reflecting the US's attitude toward immigration after the attacks. As Darren Mooney points out, "In many ways, the subtext of the eighth season mythology played to the worst excesses of post-9/11 rhetoric, particularly the tendency to treat the 'alien' as inherently hostile or dangerous."[13] In fact, hate crimes, especially against those who were thought to be Arab Muslims, increased immediately after 9/11, rising from twenty-eight during 2000 to 481 during 2001 according to the FBI.[14]

The X-Files foreshadowed not just some of the responses to 9/11, but also the conspiracy theories that arose in its wake. In particular, a "truther" movement emerging in the wake of 9/11 believed—and continues to believe—that a shadowy organization within

---

12   Cantor 2012, p. 286.

13   Mooney 2017, p. 163.

14   Singh. 2002. "'We Are Not The Enemy': Hate Crimes Against Arabs, Muslims, and Those Perceived to be Arab or Muslim after September 11." *Human Rights Watch*.

the US government was responsible for, or at the least complicit in, the September 11 attacks. Among the theories proposed by the movement: that explosives placed within the Twin Towers—and not the planes—had caused the buildings to come down; that the Bush administration had known of the attacks but did nothing; and that Israel had orchestrated the events as a false-flag operation. Bizarrely, however, the pilot episode of *The Lone Gunmen*, one of *The X-Files*'s spinoff series created by Carter, featured a plotline that mirrored the events of 9/11. In the episode, which aired on March 4, 2001, a hacker takes control of a Boeing 727 airplane with the intention of crashing the plane into the World Trade Center. Byers, Frohike, and Langly are able to prevent the attack, discovering that it was organized by a group within the United States government that had planned to blame it on foreign dictators in order to start a profitable war for the US. This is, in fact, one of the conspiracy theories that has been circulated about 9/11, and the similarity between the attacks and the episode's plot worried Carter and his fellow producers. Frank Spotnitz, when asked about the connection, said,

> We were really upset, and worried that somehow we had inspired the plot. But we were relieved to discover that the plot pre-dated *The Lone Gunmen*, and that 9/11 had nothing to do with our work. And then once we realized that, my next thought was how the government hadn't known about this plot.[15]

The American public craved reassurance after 9/11, and *The X-Files*'s declining ratings may have been in part because, as Paul A. Cantor suggests, no one wanted to acknowledge the fact that the show had predicted a new age of international terrorism and government surveillance with "uncanny accuracy." While many argued that the series had become culturally irrelevant during season nine, the two-hour finale "The Truth" highlighted the diminishing of civil liberties

---

15   Newitz. 2008. "Chris Carter Says 9/11 Killed *X-Files*, But America Is Ready for It Again." *Gizmodo*.

and suspension of legal rights that were afforded to anyone accused—or even suspected—of trying to undermine the government. "The Truth" opens with Mulder breaking into a secret military base and discovering highly classified documents that provide details about the Syndicate's plan to colonize earth in collaboration with alien forces. Interrupted and overpowered by super soldier Knowle Rohrer, Mulder manages to flips him onto high-voltage wiring, apparently killing him. In his attempt to escape, Mulder is arrested and kept in military custody, awaiting trial. Mulder's treatment in custody draws parallels to the treatment of suspects held at Guantanamo Bay on terrorism charges, revealed in a report leaked to the *New York Times* in 2004, two years after the series ended. Mulder is beaten, tortured, and denied legal counsel or the right to speak to anyone beyond the facility. When he is eventually put on trial, FBI deputy director Alvin Kersh presides over the proceedings with strict instructions to deliver a guilty verdict that will result in Mulder being sentenced to death.

This may seem like a heavy-handed way to comment on the worst excesses of the US government in the aftermath of 9/11 and throughout the war on terror, but the original ending made that commentary even clearer: then-President George W. Bush, overlooking the Washington Monument from inside the White House, is handed a note telling him that Mulder has escaped (with the help of Scully, Skinner, Doggett, Reyes, and, bizarrely, Kersh), to which he responds, "What do you want me to do? I was told this was being handled. The truth is out there now." We then pan to one of the judges we saw at Mulder's trial—identified as an alien by Gibson Praise, a child prodigy who possesses alien DNA and the ability to read minds—who replies, "The truth has always been out there, Mr. President. The people just don't want to believe."[16] This deliberate naming of a US president at the heart of a global conspiracy, at a time when the same president was responsible for enacting what were considered Orwellian measures to protect America, is striking. Rather than adopting a patriotic stance celebrating America and its leaders, as most of the media was doing at

---

16   The deleted scene and Frank Spotnitz's commentary can be found on the season nine DVD.

the time, Carter and his fellow writers maintained the subversion the series had always stood for. The fact that this was a deleted scene—which Spotnitz was happy to see cut—doesn't take away from how engaged the series was with the issues that were raised as a result of 9/11. *The X-Files* managed to stay relevant to the moment even as the rest of the media was edging away from the very questions that the show was demanding answers to. Reflecting on the end of the series some twenty years later, we can more easily see how the show was not only relevant to its time but has remained relevant over the decades that have passed. Even today *The X-Files* is a key part of the cultural landscape—referred to in articles about everything from politics to the paranormal and studied by academics and scholars in a myriad of fields—as I discuss in the next chapter.

CHAPTER 3

Reviving The X-Files in the Trump Era

"We're now living in a post-coverup, post-conspiracy age."
-Dr. They ("The Lost Art of Forehead Sweat")

By the end of the series's original run in 2002, critics felt that the show had lost its way. A combination of falling ratings, the loss of David Duchovny for most of the final two seasons, and the September 11 terrorist attacks, discussed in the last chapter, meant that there was no place for a show preoccupied with an extraterrestrial threat and a government that couldn't save its people. As Andrew Stuttaford wrote: "*The X-Files* is a product of a time that has passed. It is a relic of the Clinton years as dated as a dot-com share certificate, a stained blue dress or Kato Kaelin's reminiscences."[1] As I pointed out in the introduction, though, the show was still a part of the cultural consciousness, broadcast globally on a range of channels. A quick google search for times when its most famous motto, "The Truth Is

---

1   Stuttaford. 2002. "The Ex-Files." *National Review Online.*

Out There," appeared in news articles between 2004 and 2012 brought up over three hundred results, including articles about the release of over 4,500 UFO-related documents by the UK's Ministry of Defence, sports conspiracy theories, an American UFO conference, and a review of Nine Inch Nails' 2007 album, *Year Zero*. In comparison, "Live long and prosper" returned just over two hundred results. Research I carried out with viewers[2] both after the revival was announced and after season ten had aired show how keenly the show had remained part of the cultural lexicon, with one writing, "The cultural context of conspiracy theories has changed since the beginning of *X-Files*. Nowadays, every pseudoscience documentary uses similar soundtrack and narrative." *The X-Files*'s distinctive theme tune is used in a variety of places to suggest that something strange has happened (it's even available as a sound on TikTok), demonstrating how closely the show is linked to the idea of conspiracies. But it also hints at the negative impact the series has had in relation to the conspiracy theory movement. It's at this point that it's worth considering some of the criticisms of *The X-Files* and the nature of contemporary conspiratorial thinking.

<u>**XXX**</u>

Ahead of season ten, Carter had taken inspiration from conspiracy theories being discussed on the internet, including talk of a New World Order,[3] and in a 2015 interview with *The Guardian* pointed out that "Right now in the internet there are 500 conspiracy sites, and there are people like Tad O'Malley out here who have got the public's attention. And I'm interested in these people."[4] For some, though, it seemed as though the show had not only foretold conspiratorial thinking among the population, but actually encouraged it. As Jason

---

2   While the majority of survey respondents identified as fans of the shows, a small number of non fans (0.8 percent of the total) also completed the questionnaire.

3   Puchko. 2015. "Chris Carter and Mitch Pileggi Reflect on Conspiracies, Twitter and Return of *The X-Files*." CBR.com.

4   Dredge 2015.

Diamond writes in his article on the show's twentieth anniversary: "I'm not saying that *The X-Files* bears the majority of responsibility for that shift [in attitudes toward the government], but a television show that (at its peak) pulled in nearly 20 million viewers per episode, and took every opportunity to drive home the point that everything we believe in and take for granted is a lie, had to play some role in bringing different and potentially extreme ways of thinking to the masses."[5]

In a 2018 article for the *Straits Times*, Alison de Souza asked James Wong and Glenn and Darin Morgan if *The X-Files* had helped steer conspiracy theories into mainstream culture. Wong argued that the writers had a chance to reach a larger audience because the show was so successful: "if you're saying, 'Does that allow the audience to more readily accept conspiracies?' I guess so." But he also pointed out that conspiracy theories and those supporting them have been in existence since long before the show began. What *The X-Files* did was "tap into something that was more or less hidden in the beginning when we were doing it, but I don't believe that we're at the forefront of what's happening today."[6] Glenn Morgan agrees, saying that the conspiracy theories that circulate now are "so beyond anything we were even proposing as entertainment. You know, what InfoWars is saying. I used to check out Alex Jones back in the day and go, 'This is too weird even for us.'"[7] Fast-forward to the 2010s, however, and Alex Jones is citing *The X-Files* as having predicted COVID-19 and the conspiracy theories surrounding it. In a 2021 interview with *Paste*, Carter said, "Someone told me last night that Alex Jones was talking about how *The X-Files* actually was talking about spiked viruses long before we ever heard about the coronavirus—or were made more aware of it. I've got serious cred on Info Wars, apparently. I don't know what to

5   Diamond. 2013. "The Truth Is Still Out There: An Appreciation of *The X-Files* on Its 20th Anniversary." *Flavorwire*.

6   de Souza. 2018. "How *X-Files* brought conspiracy theories into mainstream culture." *The Straits Times*.

7   Ibid.

do with that."⁸ Given the growth of anti-intellectualism throughout the 2000s, the rise in the number of people denying climate change and its connection to human behavior, and the increasing number of conspiracy theories that support the idea that vaccines can cause autism, Carter's 'serious cred' on InfoWars is not that surprising. Mulder might have been paranoid, but he was paranoid for a reason, as we see time and time again on the show. It's not a leap to suggest that some viewers might recognize this and apply it to the real world, especially given the government abuses that came to light long after the war on terror had begun.⁹

In fact, one of the biggest criticisms aimed at the revival seasons is that the inclusion of the vaccination subplot—that the smallpox vaccination every American received would strip their immune systems, spreading the Spartan Virus and wiping out everyone who doesn't have alien DNA—was irresponsible even before the arrival of COVID-19. This use of vaccinations as a means of controlling and tracking the population, and even changing human DNA wasn't new for the show. In season three's "Paper Clip," Mulder and Scully find the Syndicate hoarding records of smallpox vaccinations and medical experiments; in season four's "Herrenvolk," Scully finds proof that smallpox vaccinations were used to catalog people; later in the same season, we find out the Russians are also developing a vaccine and are taking samples of prisoners' smallpox vaccination proteins to identify them in later experiments; the list goes on. But society had changed in the years since the show ended. Reflecting on season ten for *The Atlantic*, Sophie Gilbert, Megan Garber, David Sims, and Lenika Cruz wrote, "Vaccines? Seriously? Do you know what the public-health ramifications are of having Dana Scully (of all people!) reveal that

8   Wax. 2021. "Chris Carter on the Continued Prescience of *The X-Files*, 28 Years After Its Premiere." *Paste*.

9   A group of researchers carried out an experiment in 2018 to establish whether being exposed to conspiracy narratives would make viewers more inclined to believe in conspiracy theories. Kera Nera, Myrto Pantazi, and Oliver Klein asked 203 participants to watch an episode of *The X-Files* and answer a questionnaire about the experience and their conspiracy beliefs. They found that contrary to expectation, exposure to a conspiracy did not lead to a greater endorsement of conspiracy beliefs.

the smallpox vaccine actually contains a secret virus that allows the government to destroy our immune systems (enhanced by releasing radiation and phosphorus into the air), at which point the other vaccines we've received over time will kill us?"[10] This was echoed by many of the fans who responded to my questionnaire. The inclusion of the storyline was considered a bad idea in the current climate partly because of the reactions it evoked. One fan said they were turned off "by the way some fans overlooked the potential harm of anti-government conspiracy theories (especially involving vaccines). I felt the episodes promoted fear of government and especially government health initiatives." Another pointed out that "people are getting sick because of anti-vaccine propaganda and Carter wants to encourage them?" This last comment speaks to the rising anti-intellectualism and distrust of experts that had also emerged since the end of the show's original run (which I discuss more in Chapter Six). It is highly unlikely that Carter wants to encourage anti-vaccine propaganda—although his desire for the population to question what we are told rather than uncritically accept that the government is working in our best interests has been clear since *The X-Files*'s early days. What the revival seasons fail to understand, despite the success of Tad O'Malley, who has achieved wealth and fame through hosting a popular internet talk show, is the impact of celebrity and internet culture on the shaping of public opinion. When the paranoia we see in *The X-Files* is embraced by organizations like Infowars, positioning Scully as an apparent anti-vaxxer sends the wrong message.[11]

XXX

Despite emerging as shorthand for anything strange or weird and in spite of its focus on government subterfuge, *The X-Files* wasn't relevant

---

10   Gilbert, Garber, Sims, and Cruz. 2016. "*The X-Files*: Do We Still Want To Believe?" *The Atlantic*.

11   In the season 10 finale Scully and Einstein attempt to develop a vaccine using Scully's DNA after she realizes she is immune to the Spartan Virus following her earlier abduction. Vaccines prove to be the solution to the Virus, and Tad O'Malley even announces the existence of a vaccine on his talk show. For some, however, this was overshadowed by the foregrounding of vaccinations as the problem in the early part of the season.

THE TRUTH IS STILL OUT THERE

just in relation to pseudoscientific documentaries and conspiracy theorists. As I outlined in the introduction, the social, political, and economic landscape had changed dramatically since the series ended in 2002. The faith and trust that people had put in their governments following the 9/11 attacks and the subsequent war on terror had faded, driven by a deepening economic crisis, the weakening of privacy rights through the Patriot Act, and political scandals as well as WikiLeaks's exposure of various human rights and civil liberties violations. In an interview with Jason Davis, Carter talked about writing Mulder and Scully in a post-9/11 world, saying, "I think there are different eras of post-9/11. There was the 'near-era,' a very fearful time when we put all our faith in our government to protect us. As time has gone on, I think we are losing faith in our government and in our leaders because we feel that we are not necessarily being told the whole picture."[12] While the original iteration of *The X-Files* might have been inspired by America's involvement in the Cold War and the Watergate scandal, the 2000s had their own crises. As Adam Tooze writes, the "financial and economic crisis of 2007-2012 morphed between 2013 and 2017 into a comprehensive political and geopolitical crisis of the post–cold war order"[13]—making this a perfect time for *The X-Files* to be revived.

Carter and his cowriters dove straight in to what British writer Mark Lawson calls "a new era of governmental paranoia and public skepticism."[14] Season ten opens with the mytharc episode "My Struggle" and the return of the monologue as Mulder gives us an overview of the X-Files and a potted history of UFO sightings. After the opening title sequence (with the original credits, albeit with the inclusion of Skinner), we find Mulder watching Jimmy Kimmel online, a piece of tape obscuring his webcam. Scully calls and asks if he's been watching an online talk show host called Tad O'Malley, who believes that a global conspiracy of men has been developing

---

12   Davies. 2016. *Writing The X-Files. Interviews with Chris Carter, Frank Spotnitz, Vince Gilligan, John Shiban and Howard Gordon*. HarlanEllisonBooks.com, p.33.

13   Tooze. 2018. *Crashed: How a Decade of Financial Crises Changed the World*. Penguin, p. 20.

14   Lawson. 2016. "'Your government lies': why the *X-Files* revival is just right for our climate of extreme skepticism." *The Guardian*.

alien technology in order to take over the world, using the idea of an alien invasion as a smoke screen. So far so *X-Files*. But O'Malley is a right-wing conspiracy theorist whose online talk show, titled *The Truth Squad*, focuses on a range of fringe topics. When we're first introduced to O'Malley a video of the burning World Trade Center plays behind him as he argues that 9/11 was a false flag operation meant to pin the attacks on terrorists and that the mainstream liberal media lie to Americans about life, liberty, and the right to bear arms. In "My Struggle," O'Malley refers to the Patriot Act, introduced as part of the Bush regime's war on terror, as a tool used to "distract, enrage, and enslave American citizens at home." The obvious parallels to conspiracy theorists like Alex Jones and Glenn Beck were highlighted by scores of fans and critics. Rather than the series being too out of step to return in the late 2010s, Carter's incorporation of topics like surveillance, governments' misuse of power and methods of social control meant that season ten was very much situated in the moment.

Although the earlier seasons had used the contemporary political and cultural climate as inspiration for the events of the show, they had rarely directly commented on contemporary politics. In fact, season ten included one of only two times when a serving president was featured on *The X-Files* as more than simply a portrait hanging on the wall, as Mulder watched a Jimmy Kimmel interview with Barack Obama in "My Struggle." The other deliberate nod to a sitting president was when a photograph of George W. Bush appeared in *I Want to Believe*, accompanied by the first six notes from *The X-Files*'s theme music.[15] Seasons ten and eleven in some ways seemed *overly* political—rather than using contemporary politics as a background to the paranormal elements of the show, they placed them front and center, perhaps most overtly in season eleven, which emerged into a radically different political climate in which multiple versions of the truth existed and were embraced not just by the fringes but by many pockets of the population, politicians, and the media. With anti-vaccination sentiment, birtherism, the 9/11 truther movement

---

15   Many fans were critical of this, accusing Carter of breaking the fourth wall in order to make an unnecessary political joke.

and the flourishing of white supremacist communities in online spaces like 4chan and Reddit, it's not surprising that one fan told me, "The show was great for its time, but they're going to have to up their game considering how mainstream crazy conspiracy theories have become." The revival seasons certainly did that, particularly in season eleven's "The Lost Art of Forehead Sweat," which I focus on in Chapter Six. Carter has argued that the show approaches the current climate indirectly. Yet the themes that developed throughout seasons ten and eleven were inextricably linked to the climate in which the show reemerged and the increasing chasm between the left and right.

XXX

In his article for *Inverse*, Rowan Kaiser questions why season ten of *The X-Files* is "getting into any level of politics." He argues that on the rare occasions the original seasons deliberately "picked sides" in the political debate, "it always made that more about the specificity of the episode than a general belief that someone's conspiracy theories were right or wrong."[16] Season ten, however, aligns conspiracy theorists with the right wing, which, for Kaiser, is dangerous territory. There seems to be no reason to position Tad O'Malley, who is right in his belief that a conspiracy exists, specifically as a right-wing conspiracy theorist or to have Mulder side with him (and therefore the right wing) or pitch him in opposition to Scully. O'Malley could have just as easily been portrayed as a nonpartisan conspiracy theorist dedicated to the truth. In an interview with *Entertainment Weekly*, Carter argued that season ten was not embracing right-wing theories and that O'Malley was a character who casts *everything* in doubt.[17] The trouble with this statement is we don't really see evidence of that. O'Malley may not believe the theories he spouts on his talk show—we never get evidence that he genuinely believes what he's saying—but in a series in which the two leads have always maintained the courage of their convictions, it's

---

16   Kaiser. 2016. "What's Going On With *The X-Files'* Glenn Beck Wannabe Tad O'Malley?" *Inverse.*

17   Hibberd 2016.

difficult to trust a fictional version of right-wing conspiracy theorists who perpetuate actual harm in a milieu in which the "truth" has become confused with anti-vaccination rhetoric. The media, in the mid-2010s, was preoccupied with a wide range of controversial topics, with many platforms giving equal screen time to people on both sides of the debate. Issues being discussed during 2014 and 2015 included an increasing awareness of ISIS in the US, following airstrikes in Syria; the shootings of Michael Brown, Eric Garner, and Walter Scott by police officers and the subsequent Black Lives Matter protests; terrorist attacks in France and other European countries; mass shootings in the US, including the Charleston church shooting, which was rooted in white supremacy and led to a reevaluation of the display of the Confederate flag; and the announcement of a referendum to determine if the UK would leave the European Union. Many of these topics were heavily partisan and led to increasing friction between political parties and communities in the US and abroad. The introduction of a right-wing internet pundit who acted as an ally to Mulder, while certainly timely, was a controversial choice. But it's also a fitting one for a time when the culture wars had overtaken the war on terror. It's certainly possible to see *The X-Files* as an attempt to bridge the culture wars through Scully and Mulder, as Paul Arras does.[18] While pitted against each other as skeptic and believer, scientist and intuit, they always end up on each other's side. While Scully might find Mulder's belief in all sorts of strange phenomena maddening, and Mulder (and viewers) might find Scully's disbelief in spite of all she's seen frustrating, they are a team united against the larger forces that threaten to separate them. I think we could see Mulder's allying with O'Malley as an attempt by Carter to address the current culture wars, though possibly not a very successful one. At one point in "My Struggle," Skinner tells Mulder that "since 9/11, the country has taken a very dangerous turn in a wrong direction"—highlighting the increasing distrust in government, the increasingly outlandish conspiracy theories that have made their way from the internet to mainstream networks, and the

---

18   Arras. 2018. *The Lonely Nineties. Visions of Community in Contemporary US Television*. Springer International Publishing.

growing division between different groups within society.

"Home Again" is an episode that reflects this, asking questions about our responsibilities to each other and the impact that the art we create has on the world. In scenes that recall the Civil Rights Movement of the sixties, as well as more recent protests across the globe, the episode opens with a fire department blasting water cannons at a group of homeless people in order to clear the streets ahead of an urban renewal project being led by the US Department of Housing and Urban Development. Since the homeless people had already been ordered to move on by the department, the implication is that they have no one but themselves to blame for finding themselves soaking wet and their belongings confiscated by the clean-up crew. We follow department representative Joseph Cutler as he returns to his office, where he is unceremoniously murdered by a tall figure in a trench coat who then leaves the scene in the back of a garbage truck. This figure, given the name Band-Aid Nose Man by writer Glen Morgan, is an artist's impression come to life. Initially created by the Banksy-esque Trashman in order to give the homeless a voice, Band-Aid Nose Man is a literal embodiment of the trash that gets discarded and never thought of again. While we might, as Trashman says "throw our grande cup or our pop bottle in the right trash can under the sink, tie it in a bag, take it outside, and put it in the right dumpster," it still piles up in the landfill and leaks "toxins into the water and the sky." While perhaps a bit of a heavy-handed commentary on environmentalism and climate change, the episode also reflects how we treat each other, asking us to consider what we put out into the world both literally and metaphorically. Through his art, Trashman creates a physical being that then does his bidding in the real world. He tries to argue that he didn't mean for it to happen, that Band-Aid Nose Man used him as a conduit to assume physical form and wreak havoc on the city, in what is clearly meant as a parallel to current online discourse. Hate speech that circulates online and in the press about different groups in society, such as the anti-Muslim rhetoric since 9/11 or the current hysteria about transgender people, doesn't stay online but becomes manifest in vandalism and physical attacks. Trashman argues that "all we do is hold the pencil. All we do is hold the clay," as if the ideas that come from art can't have a real-world impact, but as Scully argues in response, "You are responsible. If you made the problem, if it was your idea . . . then you're responsible." "Home Again" points out that what we create can influence others (as we'll see in relation to *The X-Files* itself when I talk about the effect Scully had on women and girls entering fields of science, technology, engineering, and medicine later in this book). This is a timely comment given the culture wars evident in the 2010s and 2020s both in the US and across the globe.

XXX

Although *The X-Files* originally focused on American issues, the new environment it saw itself returning to in 2016 meant that it had to deal with more global concerns. Cigarette Smoking Man's desire to return the planet to its "savage state," expressed in "My Struggle III," seems to reflect the regressive theme of returning to the past, a key part of the political landscape in the mid-2010s. Trump wanted to "make America great again"; the United Kingdom called a referendum on its continued membership in the European Union in a similar attempt to take back control and return to former glory (which, I would argue, was debatable to begin with). Dealing with new conspiracy theories in the revival seasons was par for the course for the show, given that it had always engaged with the culture and politics of its time, but the explicit references to Trump in season eleven shifted the show's political commentary from general to specific. The revival was successful in highlighting *The X-Files*'s relevance to the contemporary period, including references to conspiracy movements introduced following the show's ending in 2002, increasing use of government surveillance, and the proliferation of fake news and disinformation. One fan told me they felt the revival seasons reflected the current moment, writing:

> I always thought of *The X Files* in retrospective as an (incidental?) instrument to getting people to become paranoid of their government, which is an instrument of the real powers to manipulate democracies. I feel now they owned this

conception and started focusing the enemy in the post-truth, I felt this change was particularly interesting.

And indeed, many other viewers—fans and critics both—felt the same way. However, the fact that the show managed to reflect the contemporary mood did not make the revival seasons a total success, as I talk about in the next section.

SECTION TWO

THE TRUTH IS OUT THERE

CHAPTER 4

Reality, Fiction, and Postmodernism in the Search for the Truth

"Truth is as subjective as reality."
-Jose Chung ("Jose Chung's 'From Outer Space'")

I f trusting no one is the foundation of the series, then the search for the truth is its guiding principle. In the pilot episode Scully asks Mulder to trust her, that her goal is to solve the case just like him; later, she says, "I'm here to solve this case, Mulder. I want the truth." The truth that Mulder gives her is of course that the class of 1989 is being abducted by aliens. So begins a search that asks us to consider the questions of what truth really is. I'm not a philosopher, but my brief foray into the subject at university (I did write my undergraduate philosophy dissertation on truth and reality in contemporary popular culture, using *The X-Files* as a case study) introduced me to different notions of what the truth is. Is there an objective reality—a truth that exists outside of our own perspectives? Is what we see really what is there? How do we know we're living in the "real" world and we're

THE TRUTH IS STILL OUT THERE

not just simulations in a computer game? *The X-Files* deals with these questions in various ways, but one episode that I think gets to the heart of the show is "Jose Chung's 'From Outer Space'."[1] I do need to confess my love for this episode, and it always surprises me when it appears on fans' "worst of" lists. Some of the criticisms I've heard are that it's not what the show is "really" about and that its comedy fails to hit the mark. And to some extent, perhaps, they have a point: certainly the standalone episodes of the first two seasons are not outrightly funny (with the exception of "Humbug," another Darin Morgan-penned episode) and they don't offer the postmodern reflection on the series that "Jose Chung's" does. Typical of Morgan's scripts, "Jose Chung" is more subversive than many other *X-Files* episodes, more keen to bend the reality of what we are seeing. But I maintain that "Jose Chung's" is not only one of the best episodes, it is also in many ways the epitome of what *The X-Files* is about.

From the beginning of "Jose Chung's," we are encouraged to doubt what we see. The episode opens with a shot of the underside of a spaceship moving slowly across the night sky, but seconds later, the spaceship is revealed to be a crane, with the panning camera giving it the appearance of movement. Likewise, the gray aliens we see appear to be the real thing, carrying out an abduction—that is until we hear their American accents and see their mouths moving under their masks. This opening sets the theme for the episode and reiterates the conceit of the show as a whole: truths are buried beneath truths, and we never know if what we're seeing can actually be believed. Scully and Jose Chung, discussing the events of Klass County after the opening credits, give us a further indication as to the notions of truth we will see in the episode:

SCULLY: Well, just as long as you're attempting to record the truth.
JOSE CHUNG: Oh, God, no. How can I possibly do that? [. . .] I spent three months in Klass County, and

---

1   If you're interested in philosophy, I would recommend *The Philosophy of The X-Files*, edited by Dean A. Kowalski (2007) and *The X-Files and Philosophy: The Truth Is in Here* edited by Robert Arp (2017). Both of these cover far more topics, in far more detail, than I ever could.

everybody there has a different version of what truly happened.

Here, we see Chung expounding a traditional metaphysical claim that philosopher Immanuel Kant also subscribed to: there is the way that the world really is and the way that the world *appears* to us. Everyone has a different version of the world, of the events that happened in Klass County (and in the series more broadly), and everyone believes those versions to be true. "Jose Chung's" cleverly makes the point that we can never get past the way that things appear to us, and our knowledge is of only the appearance of things (the reality that we see), not things as they really are (the truth). In this way, "Jose Chung's" is also referring to the nature of truth in *The X-Files*: that the truth changes, depending on who's telling us what happened.

Take Samantha's disappearance, for example. From the beginning of the series, we are told that she was abducted by aliens, that this was the driving force behind Mulder's entry to the FBI and the discovery of the X-Files. As the series progresses, however, we get told different truths about what actually happened to her up (which we may be able to pass off as continuity errors on the part of the writers, but still, they are presented to us on the show as true events). In "Little Green Men," we see that Samantha was taken from the living room while she and Mulder played Stratego (in earlier episodes, such as "Conduit," we were told that she was taken from her bed); in "The Blessing Way," we are told that she isn't dead—or at least not dead in the same way that Bill Mulder now is; in "Paper Hearts," the suggestion is that she was taken from her home by John Lee Roche and killed; in "Closure," we are told that she is dead, taken by the walk-ins and traveling through time in starlight. We also see different truths relating to Samantha's growing up. In "Colony," we are told she was returned and placed with an adoptive family (whom Samantha refers to as aliens) who raised her as their daughter; in "Redux II," we are told Samantha was taken to Cigarette Smoking Man, who was referred to as her father, and grew up to have children of her own; in "Closure," we are told that she lived with Cigarette Smoking Man and that tests were performed on her before she ran away. Morgan plays with the idea of truth in "Jose

Chung's" to make us question the notion of truth we are presented with in the series. The truth on *The X-Files*, much like the truth in "Jose Chung's" is revealed to us slowly—when it is revealed at all. Take, for example, Deep Throat. Explaining why he can't reveal who his source is to Scully in "E.B.E," Mulder says of him, "He's never lied to me. I won't break that confidence. I trust him"—only for his trust to be subverted later on when Mulder realizes the photographic evidence Deep Throat gave him is fake.

Mulder's ability to believe the different truths shown to him about his sister's disappearance, about the people he can trust, is reflected on a smaller scale in the different truths shown to us about what happened in Klass County. In that respect I think we can see "Jose Chung's" as a microcosm of the show as a whole. Much like Mulder comes to realize that the truths he was brought up with are in fact lies, the viewer sees newer "truths" being introduced as Harold and Chrissy change their stories, reflecting the shifting nature of the truth seen throughout the show. Initially, Chrissy's story is that Harold raped her, which changes to a typical abduction experience:

> CHRISSY GIORGIO: I'm in a room . . . on a spaceship . . .
> surrounded by aliens.
> FINGERS: What do the aliens look like?
> CHRISSY GIORGIO: They're small . . . but their heads
> and their eyes are big. They're gray.

Which later develops into a CIA cover-up:

> CHRISSY GIORGIO: Some men are lifting me off the
> ground . . . men in Air Force uniforms.
> MULDER: Air Force?
> FINGERS: Where are you now, Chrissy?
> CHRISSY GIORGIO: I'm in a room. In an office. I'm
> surrounded by men. Some are in uniforms, some are
> in suits.

Hypnosis is a recurring theme throughout the early seasons of the show, with Mulder revealed to have undergone regression hypnosis in "Conduit" in order to discover what happened to Samantha and going

under again in "The Field Where I Died" to recover his past lives.
Scully too is hypnotized, in "The Red and the Black," to access her lost
memories. Memories and dreams are often offered up by the series as
a way to come to the truth of a matter (as Mulder says in "Aubrey":
"I've often felt that dreams are answers to questions we haven't yet
figured out how to ask"), yet the truths they offer are always subject
to scrutiny. Like the thoughts and memories of Mulder in "The Sixth
Extinction II" (which I talk about in the next chapter), they may be
the product of a force that implants false ideas and memories in our
minds. A person's mind is easily malleable, subject to suggestion and
fiction. Ed Jerse in "Never Again" kills because of a talking tattoo—
something we later discover is actually caused by ergot poisoning,
and Robert Modell, in "Pusher," is able to convince people to do his
bidding through the power of suggestion. Even Scully, in "Wetwired,"
falls victim to subliminal messaging that leads to her nearly shooting
Mulder. Under hypnosis, as we see in "Jose Chung's," autosuggestion
becomes a real possibility—a fact that Scully acknowledges: "I know
that it has its therapeutic value, but it has never been proven to
enhance memory. In fact, it actually worsens it, since, since, since
people in that state are prone to confabulation." We never get to the
truth in "Jose Chung's"—we just get versions of it. Mulder's, Scully's,
Roky's, Chrissy's—each depends on their own subjective experience
rather than an objective or real truth. And this mirrors the series itself.

XXX

The nature of the truth discovered on *The X-Files* is never clear and
always open to interpretation. Part of that is because of whose eyes
we're seeing the truth through. From the very beginning of the show,
Scully is established as the audience's lens through which to see *The
X-Files*. She's the first of the two main leads we're introduced to
when we see her arrive at FBI headquarters and enter Section Chief
Blevins's office. We're also given her credentials and some of her
background before Mulder is even introduced, finding out that she
attended medical school, from where she was recruited into the FBI—
something her parents still think of as an act of rebellion. Although

brief, this introduction tells the audience that we are aligned with this character—she is our introduction to the world of the X-Files. As scholar Lacy Hodges points out:

> In the pilot episode, Scully is established as the series' connection to the rational and the real. She enters the series at the same place and time as the viewer—the viewer, like Scully, is expecting to "debunk the X-Files project." She is the original screen surrogate and, through access to her inner thoughts as projected by the case reports that she writes while investigating with Mulder, she serves as the voice with which the viewer can originally identify.[2]

This was something that Carter intended from the beginning. "Scully's point of view is the point of view of the show," he told Rolling Stone magazine. "And so the show has to be built on a solid foundation of science, in order to have Mulder take a flight from it."[3] From this perspective, the audience is meant to identify with Scully and, as Joe Bellon argues, "join in her quest to determine if Mulder is right about the existence of extra-terrestrials."[4] In the pilot episode, we hear Scully's version of events in a voice-over as she's typing on her laptop. Although she apparently experienced the same period of lost time that Mulder did, she writes in her report that "Agent Mulder's insistence of time loss due to unknown forces cannot be validated or substantiated by this witness." Scully is a scientist, and her belief in science affects the way she views the events of the show. Discussing Karen Swenson's death in the pilot, she says:

> The girl obviously died of something. If it was natural causes, it's plausible that there was something missed in the post mortem. If she was murdered, it's plausible

---

2   Hodges. 2005. *"Scully, What Are You Wearing?": The Problem of Feminism, Subversion, and Heteronormativity in The X-Files.* MA Diss. University of Florida, p. 14.

3   Lipsky. 1997. "The Virtue of Paranoia." *Rolling Stone.*

4   Bellon. 1999. "The strange discourse of *The X-Files*: What it is, what it does, and what is at stake." *Critical Studies in Media Communication* 16.2, p. 150.

there was a sloppy investigation. What I find fantastic is any notion that there are answers beyond the realm of science. The answers are there. You just have to know where to look.

And look Scully does. Whenever Mulder presents a paranormal explanation to a case, Scully counters with a rational justification based on science and logic rather than intuition or faith. Carter has called Mulder's faith in the paranormal "tantamount to a religious belief,"[5] and this affects the way he views "the truth"—frequently in opposition to what Scully thinks. Yet in actuality the two have to work together to find a truth that exists "not in opposition but in partnership."[6] A perfect example of this duality is evident in "Bad Blood," another of my favorite episodes. It's brilliantly funny, but it also acts something like a spiritual successor to "Jose Chung's" in the way it reflects on truth, subjectivity, and whether seeing really is believing.

Written by Vince Gilligan, who seemed to take over as the comedy writer after Darin Morgan, the episode opens with a teenage boy running through the woods at night. He falls and is jumped on by the man pursuing him, who holds the boy down and rams a wooden stake through his chest. Of course, the pursuer is Mulder, who is eventually caught up to by Scully, who's horrified at what he's done. Mulder opens the boy's mouth to reveal fangs, which promptly fall out when Scully taps them. Skinner, understandably, wants an explanation, as the family of the murdered boy—Ronnie Strickland—is suing the FBI for $446 million. While both Mulder and Scully are planning to tell him what they saw, they have conflicting ideas of what exactly happened—highlighted to great effect with the portrayal of Sheriff Lucius Hartwell. Thus, the premise of the episode is set. Scully tells us her version of events first, in which Mulder jumps to paranormal conclusions about the nature of the case (classic vampirism) and scorns the more rational explanation that "ritualistic bloodletting points towards cultists of some sort." In Scully's version of events,

5   Rhodes. 2008. "Q&A: Chris Carter of *The X-Files*." *Smithsonian Magazine*.

6   Hansen. "Catholicism in *The X-Files*: Dana Scully and the harmony of faith and reason." *Science Fiction Film and Television 6.1* (2013) p. 58.

Mulder is dismissive (he makes quotation marks with his fingers when referring to her "theories"), disrespectful (he storms into her motel room covered in mud, climbs onto the bed, and orders her to conduct a second autopsy), and dramatic (demanding the sheriff immediately take him to "an old cemetery in town off the beaten path, the creepier the better"). Scully, in contrast, is calm and rational—offering a theory that the murderer might believe himself to be a vampire and listing a range of "genetic afflictions which cause a heightened sensitivity to light, to garlic—porphyria, xeroderma pigmentosum." She is a consummate professional, forgoing both dinner and sleep in order to conduct a second autopsy at Mulder's request. In Mulder's version, Scully is the one who's dismissive. When he tells her his theory about the case, that what they may be looking at is what *appears* to be a series of vampire or *vampire*-like attacks, he adds that he's very eager to hear her opinion. Scully's response is "Well, it's obviously not a vampire. Because they don't exist?" given in a way that clearly suggests Mulder is the crazy one for even suggesting that. Mulder, for his part, is submissive and deferential to Scully and acknowledges that his methods may seem a little off (to which the sheriff replies that Mulder works for the government and runs the show—not the usual response to Mulder's theories).

Before they can tell Skinner their stories, Mulder and Scully are ordered back to Texas, where the coroner who was going to perform the autopsy has been "gnawed on." There, they establish that perhaps elements of both of their stories are true—while it really was a vampire responsible for the deaths, it may have been a vampire who had watched too many Dracula movies. In his review of the episode, Robert Shearman argues that what makes it clever is "the way that the agents aren't just portrayed as each other's polar opposites."[7] In some obvious respects they are, but in less obvious ways they're far more similar than perhaps either of them would let on. For a start, they are both seekers of the truth, regardless of whatever that truth might ultimately be. Rodney F. Hill, in his article on the impossibility

---

7   Shearman 2009, p. 136.

of knowing in *The X-Files*, points out that the two incarnate "two different approaches to seeking the truth—or two different versions of truth—at once at odds with each other and inextricably intertwined,"[8] while Regina Hansen argues that Mulder's and Scully's views on how to find the truth "exist not in opposition but in partnership."[9] This is clearly evident in "Bad Blood." Scully's scientific knowledge allows her to discover the chloral hydrate that Ronnie was using to drug his victims, while Mulder's knowledge of vampire lore means he can save himself from being attacked by Ronnie until Scully arrives. The truth requires both of them to work together. The truth we find in monster-of-the-week episodes like "Bad Blood" seems to be a different kind of truth from the one Mulder and Scully seek to uncover throughout the course of the series, however, even though the approach the two agents take is similar in both.

XXX

When Carter originally pitched the show to Fox, the network didn't like the ambiguity: "they wanted everything wrapped up; they wanted the unexplained explained."[10] That goes counter to both the stories of the paranormal that Carter sometimes drew on for inspiration and the narrative format of *The X-Files*. I talked in the introduction about how the show merged two different kinds of storyline—the standalone monster of the week and the ongoing mytharc that dealt with the conspiracy. While it was possible for the former to be explained at the end of each episode—with a final scene that suggested maybe, just maybe, things hadn't quite been concluded—it was more difficult to do it with the latter. Serial narratives, which *The X-Files* is an example of, sometimes rely on the "truth" being hinted at or touched upon only for it to be discovered that what we've been shown is just a part

---

8   Hill. 2012. "'I Want to Believe the Truth Is Out There': *The X-Files* and the Impossibility of Knowing." In Jay P. Telotte and Gerald Duchovny (eds), *Science Fiction Film, Television, and Adaptation: Across The Screens*. Routledge, p. 123.

9   Hansen 2013, p. 58.

10   Davis 2016, p. 21.

of the whole. As Deep Throat tells Mulder in "E.B.E.," a lie is most convincingly hidden between two truths, and the actual structure of the show proves this point. In correspondence with Rodney F. Hill, scholar J. P. Telotte has suggested that the show's "The Truth Is Out There" tagline "constitutes an effective promise/premise for a form bound up in seriality, since it can always take us towards that 'truth' and then swerve off or pull back—and indeed that swerving is what keeps the series going."[11] So while the audience might get some payoff, in terms of explanations being offered in the standalone episodes, and occasional glimpses of what is "really" happening in the overarching conspiracy, the truth is never truly revealed. And going back to the episode that started this chapter, "Jose Chung's" tells us that.

Academics have argued that *The X-Files* is a postmodern show, featuring as it does complex narrative structures with multiple storylines, flashbacks and flashforwards, and references to other genres, folklore, and contemporary events.[12] "Jose Chung's" epitomizes this, arguing that humanity is always alone and the truth is essentially unknowable. This is all true. But "Jose Chung's" is also, at its core, about love. While it can be argued that this theme takes somewhat of a back seat to Chung's quest to know the intellectual truth of the events in Klass County, it is there nonetheless. The episode begins with Harold declaring his love for Chrissy and ends with his declaration that he still loves her; Roky discovers that the way to enlightenment is through love (or lust at least); Chrissy discovers a more selfless kind of love in devoting herself to improving the world. In this respect "Jose Chung's" reflects the bigger questions raised by the wider show— rather than a search for truth, it's a search for meaning, a search to find our place in the universe. As Chung himself says:

> Then there are those who care not about
> extraterrestrials, searching for meaning in other
> human beings. Rare or lucky are those who find it. For

---

11 Hill 2012, p. 118.

12 For a more detailed analysis of this, Douglas Kellner's article "*The X-Files* and the Aesthetics and Politics of Postmodern Pop" is an excellent read, while Jan Delasara's book *PopLit, PopCult and The X-Files* looks at the debates that have risen about the show's relationship to postmodernism.

although we may not be alone in the universe, in our own separate ways on this planet, we are all alone.

Chung here takes the existentialist view that we are all alone; we perceive the world through a veil of experience, opinion, and belief that no one else shares. And the episode illustrates that perfectly: the events in Klass County differ according to each teller because each experienced different things. But *The X-Files* ultimately doesn't enforce Chung's opinion. Meaning is sought after in a variety of ways—through scientific knowledge, religious experience, and other people—as we'll see in the next chapter.

CHAPTER 5

Science, Faith, and Love

*"Rattlesnakes and medieval visions of damnation.
Well, I for one feel a whole lot closer to God."
-Scully ("Signs and Wonders")*

Chris Carter once said that he saw *The X-Files* as a search for God, saying "it was a big part of the inspiration, but no one religion was the focus" and that Mulder's "I Want to Believe" poster summed it up best.[1] Certainly, there are plenty of references to religions and spiritualities (of all kinds) over the original nine seasons of the show. From Christianity to Indigenous rituals, Judaism, and Feng Shui, both Western and Eastern religions, philosophies, and ways of life are used to encourage the characters, and the audience, to question what they see, to question what they are told, and to believe that the truth is out there. I talked in the last chapter about Scully's role as the lens through which the audience views the show, and there is a certain contradiction inherent in Scully's belief systems and ways of understanding the world. On the one hand, she's a scientist, using

---

1   CBR Staff. 2008. "WonderCon: *X-Files* Panel." ..

facts to determine the truth of an event; on the other, she's a Christian whose faith, while it might have lapsed a bit (in "Revelations" she admits she hasn't been to confession in six years), is integral to the way she views the world. She wears a golden cross around her neck that her mother gave her at the age of fifteen, and she believes that God can create miracles. Her journey throughout the course of *The X-Files* could be seen to mirror that of the Virgin Mary—the birth of Emily and William's conception mirroring the immaculate conception. This dichotomy between science and religion, knowledge and faith, lies at the heart of the show and its search for truth, but it's also a point of contention: if Scully can believe in a God, then why can't she believe in the paranormal events she's witnessed so many of? In fact, it's not until Mulder is abducted and John Doggett joins the hunt for him in season eight that Scully moves from her position of paranormal skeptic to believer, changing the dynamic of the show and the lens through which we, the audience, view it.

Scholar Paul C. Peterson argues that religion isn't a main theme in the show and is not a part of most episodes, though I'd argue that it certainly plays a key part in setting up the show's premise and its broad questions of faith, belief, and truth. Carter backs this up, saying the show "dealt with faith, not religion with a capital 'R' or Catholicism with a capital 'C.'" To me, the idea of faith is really the backbone of the entire series—faith in your own beliefs, ideas about the truth, and so it has religious undertones always."[2] While these undertones exist in the early seasons, they become more pronounced at the end of season six and throughout season seven. The season six finale, "Biogenesis," opens with Scully, in a voice-over, contemplating the origin, and purpose, of life on Earth: "What no one can say for certain is what or who ignited that original spark. Is there a plan, a purpose or a reason to our existence? Will we pass, as those before us, into oblivion, into the sixth extinction that scientists warn is already in progress? Or will the mystery be revealed through a sign, a symbol, a revelation?" The question is explicitly religious, and in the episode

---

2   Lowry. 1996. *Trust No One: The Official Third Season Guide to The X Files.* Harper Collins, p. 139.

that follows we see the alien craft that was uncovered bearing symbols from different myths and religions as well as scientific discoveries. The second episode of season seven, however, is one of the more obvious episodes to use the themes of religion, symbolism, and sacrifice to get closer to the truth.

XXX

In "Bioegenesis," Mulder is committed to a psychiatric hospital after being exposed to the alien artifact Scully found. "The Sixth Extinction II: Amor Fati" opens with Mulder's mother leaving her son lying in a hospital bed, crying out for her with a voice she can't hear. We're drawn into making a comparison to Mary, mother of Jesus, who wept at the cross for the son who has to die, but while we might argue that Mary is passing her son into the arms of his father—God—who will care for him and reward him with a seat at his right hand, Mrs. Mulder passes her son into the arms of someone much more sinister—Cigarette Smoking Man, whom Carter once referred to as the Devil. Cigarette Smoking Man arrives at Mulder's bedside and injects him with a liquid that allows Mulder to move, telling him, "You've suffered enough—for the X-Files, for your partner, for the world. You're not Christ. You're not Prince Hamlet. You're not even Ralph Nader. You can walk out of this hospital and the world will forget you. Arise." The parallels with Christ are obvious here, not just in Cigarette Smoking Man's use of the name but also in the biblical stories that saw Jesus raising men from the dead. As always with Cigarette Smoking Man, however, things aren't entirely as they seem. With his arrival, we—and Mulder—are thrown into an altered reality, a dream sequence mirroring that of Martin Scorsese's *The Last Temptation of Christ*. Much like Scorsese's Christ, Mulder is offered the chance to "come down from the cross" and lead a normal life. As scholar Amy M. Donaldson points out in her analysis of the episode:

> Cigarette Smoking Man, echoing the words of the guardian angel that appears to Jesus while on the cross, tells Mulder that he has suffered enough; he is not the Christ . . . Mimicking the

angel, Cigarette Smoking Man takes his hand and leads him away from the scene of his suffering. Thus begins Mulder's greatest temptation.[3]

There are quite clear parallels throughout the rest of the episode with the film: Mulder is taken to a house where he meets Deep Throat, who tells him he can let go of the guilt he feels for those who died serving his search for the truth: "I'm here to tell you that you're not the hub of the universe, the cause of life and death. We, you and I, we're merely puppets in a master plan. No more, no less. You've suffered enough. Now you should enjoy your life." What follows are several sequences showing Mulder adapting to this new life; living with Diana Fowley and meeting his sister, who is alive and living with Cigarette Smoking Man. Yet in reality Mulder is in an operating room on a table that, lit from below, appears in the shape of a cross. On his head is a monitoring device with probes attached to his skull, clearly emulating the crown of thrones. Mulder, who is revealed to be half-alien, half-human, is the key to humanity's salvation—much like Christ—and like Christ he may have to pay the ultimate sacrifice:

> CIGARETTE SMOKING MAN: The fact remains, he's become our savior. He's immune to the coming viral apocalypse. He's the hero here.
> PROJECT DOCTOR: He may not survive the procedure.
> CIGARETTE SMOKING MAN: Then he suffers a hero's fate.

Sacrifice is a key theme in *The X-Files*. Bill Mulder sacrificed his daughter for the sake of humanity; Mulder sacrificed Scully's health, Deep Throat, and a normal life for his work on the X-Files; Scully sacrificed her relationship with her brother and her sister's life to support Mulder. In "Amor Fati," those sacrifices are deemed minor, insignificant. Mulder cannot change the world—he is merely a small cog in a tiny machine. Of course, the reality is very different. Having

---

3   Donaldson. 2007. "The Last Temptation of Mulder: Reading *The X-Files* through the Christological Lens of Nikos Kazantzakis." In Sharon R. Yang (ed.) *The X-Files and Literature: Unweaving the Story, Unraveling the Lie to Find the Truth*. Cambridge Scholars, p. 6.

learned what happened to his sister, Mulder accepts the life that Cigarette Smoking Man is offering him—the dream life in which all of the things he has lost, all of the things that have been sacrificed for the X-Files's cause, can be found just around the corner. Yet while he is living that life, the world is going to ruin. As we see snippets of his wedding day, the birth of his first child, we also see Mulder becoming older and more feeble until he is unable to move from his bed. It's at this point that Scully, mirroring her journey to find Mulder in the real world, enters the dreamscape. The apocalypse is happening outside, fire raining down from the sky and an alien craft flying overhead, and Scully is furious. Echoing the words of Judas in *The Last Temptation of Christ*, she berates Mulder, calling him a traitor, a deserter and a coward and demanding that he "get up and fight the fight." Scully tells Mulder that he isn't supposed to die "in a comfortable bed with the Devil outside," and in the real world, Mulder wakes up, asking Scully to help him. As ever, Scully comes to Mulder's rescue, bringing him back into the real world from his operating table crucifix. Donaldson argues that Scully is closer to the portrayal of Judas in *The Last Temptation of Christ*:

> In "The Sixth Extinction II: Amor Fati," Scully is Kazantzaki's Judas, right down to the blue eyes and red hair. She is the loyal friend who speaks the truth at all costs, more concerned with Mulder's quest than with his feelings. Like this Judas, Scully was sent by Mulder's enemies . . . but she was caught up in his charisma and integrity to become his closest companion.[4]

Scully, like Jesus's followers, is called on to sacrifice a normal life—dates and family time, her sister, her ability to have children—for Mulder's quest. Yet it's also Scully who forces Mulder to see that the dream he is in is not the real world and he is needed here to find the truth. Thanks to Scully, Mulder overcomes his temptation, yet Scully's beliefs are shaken in the process. At the end of the episode, she tells

---

4   Ibid p.19.

Mulder, "I don't know what to believe anymore. I was so determined to find a cure to save you that I could deny what it was that I saw, and now I don't even know what the truth is." After six seasons of Scully denying the paranormal, "Amor Fati" becomes a turning point, shaping the final three seasons of the show and the search for the truth.

XXX

We see this in another season seven episode that examines the life not lived, though this time from Scully's point of view and through the ideas of Buddhism. Duchovny wrote "Amor Fati" with the idea of exploring the decisions Mulder has made, saying:

> People ask, "when is Mulder going to get a personal life?" Well, this is the equation. This is what it's all about. Mulder is a guy who's been given the same problem. You either have a life or you sacrifice it all and you become this guy who's running around chasing aliens and has no life. I wasn't saying Mulder is Christ; I'm not inflating Mulder. What I'm doing is using the very human model of Christ to make Mulder an everyman.[5]

In a similar way, Gillian Anderson wrote "all things" as a character study for Scully, drawing on her own interests in Buddhism and spiritual healing. The episode focuses on the choices Scully has made that have brought her to this point in her life and asks what can happen when we open ourselves up to new ways of knowing. While Mulder heads off to investigate crop circles in England, Scully reconnects with her former professor Daniel Waterston—with whom, it is implied, she had an affair—after a series of coincidences that brings her to his hospital room. Waterston is suffering from an undiagnosed heart condition, and seeing him makes Scully consider whether she should have stayed in medicine and chosen a life with him rather than entering the FBI.

---

5   Vitaris. 2002. "David Duchovny on "The Unnatural" and "Hollywood A.D."" *Morgan and Wong Online.*

Mulder, via a phone call during which Scully narrowly avoids being in a car accident, asks her to meet a contact of his, Colleen Azar. Scully arranges to meet Colleen at the American Taoist Healing Center but realizes they have already met, in another coincidence, when Scully entered the wrong room at the hospital. Recognising that Scully is shaken after her experience on the road, Colleen tells her, "There is a greater intelligence in all things. Accidents—or near accidents—often remind us that we need to keep our mind open to the lessons it gives," and she advises her to slow down. While initially dismissive, Scully returns to apologize to Colleen the following day and admits that she was hoping to find answers to a "strange feeling" she had about Waterston's illness. This is clearly a departure for the levelheaded, rational Scully. There are other times throughout the series when she has felt or seen something she couldn't explain—the vision of her father in "Beyond The Sea" being perhaps the most obvious—but those have been linked to her Christian faith. For Scully to approach anything other than science or the religion she grew up in seems remarkably out of character. And this is perhaps the point of the episode. While it allows Anderson room to explore ideas she is interested in personally, it also represents room for growth in a character who has, for much of the past seven years, changed very little.

Scully's rationality and faith in science are important elements of *The X-Files*, but they also become increasingly frustrating when she fails to see—or accept—paranormal explanations for events. As much as I, and all fans, love Scully and recognize how important it is for her to act as a foil for Mulder, there are only so many times I can listen to her trying to defend a rational, scientific explanation for something that is clearly neither rational nor scientific. While "all things" might seem like a giant leap for Scully, who takes a spiritual healer to Waterston's bedside following a vision she experiences in a Buddhist temple, it continues some of the themes explored in "Biogenesis" and "Amor Fati." In the final episode of season six, Scully says, "Or will the mystery be revealed through a sign, a symbol, a revelation?" Signs and symbols run through "all things," from the Moby song that's repeated during the episode to the woman wearing a baseball cap and even the use of slow-motion. These signs ultimately lead Scully to a temple, where she has a vision telling her what is wrong with Waterston. The alien craft in "Biogenesis" includes symbols from all religions, not just Christianity, and it seems a fair assumption to make that Scully has been pondering this—as well as her relationship with Mulder—for much of season seven. That the scientific response to Waterson's heart stopping puts him in a coma but the alternative healing performed on his chakras revives him makes another crack in Scully's worldview that science offers the answers to everything. In this case—and for much of *The X-Files*—it doesn't, and it seems that only now Scully is coming to this realization. "all things" shows Scully her biases and allows her to admit to them—as we see when she tells Colleen, "I'm sorry that I was rude before. I'm a medical doctor and a scientist, and you're right, I don't know what it is that you do. But there was something that you said that I wanted to ask you about." Scully's willingness to accept other possibilities in "all things" is a marked contrast to "Beyond the Sea," where at the end of the episode she reverts to her rational self, coming up with explanations other than being psychic for why Boggs might have been right. When Mulder asks her why, with all that she has seen, she can't believe, Scully's response is "I'm afraid to believe." Yet by the end of "all things," Scully is no longer afraid to believe, or to open herself up to extreme possibilities. At the end of the episode, Mulder and Scully are sitting in Mulder's apartment discussing the events of the last few days:

MULDER: I just find it hard to believe.
SCULLY: What part?
MULDER: The part where I go away for two days and your whole life changes.
SCULLY: Mmm, I didn't say my whole life changed.
MULDER: You speaking to God in a Buddhist temple. God speaking back.
SCULLY: Mmm, and I didn't say that God spoke back. I said that I had some kind of a vision.
MULDER: Well, for you, that's like saying you're having David Crosby's baby . . . What is it?
SCULLY: I once considered spending my whole life with this man. What I would have missed.
MULDER: I don't think you can know. I mean, how many different lives would we be leading if we made

different choices. We, we don't know.
SCULLY: What if there was only one choice and all the other ones were wrong? And there were signs along the way to pay attention to.
MULDER: Mmm. And all the choices would then lead to this very moment. One wrong turn, and we wouldn't be sitting here together. Well, that says a lot. That says a lot, a lot, a lot. That's probably more than we should be getting into at this late hour.

Scully at this point has fallen asleep, but telling Mulder about the vision she had and that it had caused her to think differently about her life and her choices shows the significance of the episode to Scully's worldview and how it can—or maybe has already—changed.

XXX

We see this change most obviously in seasons eight and nine. Mulder is abducted at the end of season seven, and Special Agent John Doggett is introduced in "Within," the first episode of season eight, as part of the task force created to look for him. Doggett is a no-nonsense FBI agent who was a Marine and a member of the NYPD. Demoted to joining the X-Files after failing to find Mulder, Doggett is very much the skeptic, while Scully has begun to adopt Mulder's role as believer. In "Without," she tells Doggett that she's "seen things, things that I can't explain" before confirming that the man Doggett saw walk off a cliff was not Mulder but an alien bounty hunter transformed to look like him, searching for Gibson Praise, who is part alien. Incredulous, Doggett tells Scully, "You're, uh, you're starting to remind me a lot of Agent Mulder yourself." While Doggett was designed as a replacement for Mulder, they are clearly polar opposites. Carter, in an interview with National Public Radio, said, "What he brings is a different approach to *The X-Files*. First of all, he's a knee-jerk skeptic, so he couldn't be more different than the character of Mulder. He's an insider at the FBI, well-liked, has buddies. Mulder, of course, he's been banished to the basement along with all of his X-Files."[6] Doggett essentially takes on Scully's former role as skeptic, leaving Scully to become what Carter calls "something of a reluctant believer."[7] We see this even more clearly in "Patience" as Scully and Doggett investigate a series of gruesome murders. At the beginning of the episode, Scully takes control of the projector, in a scene that mirrors a scene from the pilot episode, and throughout the episode adopts what was typically Mulder's behavior, for example in this exchange:

> DOGGETT: The more basic answer is what we're dealing with here is simply a man. A psychotic killer with a deformed foot. You're familiar with the principle of Occam's Razor?
> SCULLY: Yeah. You take every possible explanation and you choose the simplest one. Agent Mulder used to refer to it as "Occam's Principle of Limited Imagination." Unless you have a simple explanation as to how a killer with a deformed foot leaves a print only every twenty-five feet.

Scully maintains her trust in science, but as she says in "Patience," she's a "scientist who happens to have seen a lot." This doesn't mean that she will immediately accept every alternative explanation—she is skeptical of Reyes's numerology in "Improbable," but by the end of that episode, she is curious enough to ask what her number is. Reyes tells her it's nine, completion: ""You've evolved through the experiences of all the other numbers to a spiritual realization that this life is only part of a larger whole." Much like many of the other episodes in the last three seasons of the show, "Improbable" deals with questions about fate and free will, and this is where we come back to the themes alluded to in "Jose Chung's" as well as "Amor Fati" and "all things."

The conversation at the end of "all things" clearly suggests that it's fate that brought Mulder and Scully together: the episode actually opens

---

6   Fresh Air. 2001. "Interview With Chris Carter." *National Public Radio.*

7   Ibid.

with Scully getting dressed in front of a mirror, Mulder lying asleep in the bed behind her, before flashing back to a few days earlier. The implication is that Mulder and Scully had slept together—thrilling all the shippers in the fandom—but when coupled with the overarching questions about religion and fate, I think it actually speaks to a larger truth: that there is meaning to be found in other people if only we are open to those possibilities. This is what Mulder and Scully ultimately discover. By the season nine finale, Mulder and Scully have found love with each other (something many fans thought had happened much earlier in the series), and Frank Spotnitz, in a *Science Fiction Weekly* interview, argues that this is perhaps the ultimate truth:

> The final scene addresses this head on. You can't get the truth. You can't. There's a larger truth, though: that you can't harness the forces of the cosmos, but you may find somebody else. You may find another human being. That may be kind of corny and all of that, but that's really it: Love is the only truth we can hope to know, as human beings. That's what Mulder and Scully found after nine years. And that's a lot.[8]

Think for a moment about how "The Truth" ends. Mulder and Scully have found the truth that they've spent the last nine years searching for: They know that the date is set for colonization; they know the conspiracy is real. Everything Mulder has believed has become true, and Scully has been convinced of that truth along the way as well. But the end of "The Truth" is ultimately about more than that:

> MULDER: I believe that I sat in a motel room like this with you when we first met, and I tried to convince you of the truth. And in that respect, I succeeded, but in every other way I've failed.
> SCULLY: You've always said that you want to believe. But believe in what, Mulder? If this is the truth that you've been looking for, then what is left to believe in?
> MULDER: I want to believe that the dead are not lost to

---

8   Perenson. 2001. "Frank Spotnitz tells the truth about the latest season of *The X-Files*." *Science Fiction Weekly*.

us. That they speak to us as part of something greater than us—greater than any alien force. And if you and I are powerless now, I want to believe that if we listen to what's speaking, it can give us the power to save ourselves.
SCULLY: Then we believe the same thing.

Even if you accept the idea in "Jose Chung's" that we are all ultimately alone, "The Truth" shows us that love is still real, and possibly the only way we can get close to knowing an ultimate truth. Mulder and Scully, at the end of the series, believe in the same thing. As *The X-Files* shows us time and time again, there is no one definitive truth that can be agreed upon by each party. But there are other truths. It's why Darin Morgan goes back to love in "Jose Chung's": we may not be able to agree on whether the aliens are real or not, on whether Chrissy was raped, on whether Mulder and Scully were men in black, but we can agree on love. It's why Spotnitz says it might be corny, but it's all we've got. Love is the closest we can come to knowing that ultimate truth: that even if we can't agree on what happened, we can agree that we love each other. We can sense a deeper reality by developing that closeness with other people, and we can share their perceptions and see the world maybe a little more clearly. It's what Mulder and Scully spent nine years doing, after all.

CHAPTER 6

Post-Truth, Fake News, and the Malleability of Memory

"You believe what you want to believe—that's what everybody does now."
- Dr. They ("The Lost Art of Forehead Sweat")

When it was announced that *The X-Files* would return to our TV screens in 2016, websites proclaimed that the truth was *still* out there. But the nature of truth seemed to have changed in the years since the series ended. Rather than *the* truth being out there, multiple truths seemed to be both out there and within ourselves. As anti-intellectualism continues to rise, we are encouraged to distrust the experts and rely on our own research—which is often limited to our own filter bubbles, where our existing ideas are reinforced. Anecdotes abound, often given the same credence as verified data, and misinformation spreads faster than the truth can get its boots on.

If "Jose Chung's" gets to the heart of the questions the show asked in its first nine seasons, taking the very postmodern approach that there is no knowable truth and that the best we can hope for is to find someone to share our truths with, "The Lost Art of Forehead Sweat" epitomizes the culture that had emerged by the time seasons ten and eleven were airing. Season eleven in particular was firmly situated in the era of post-truth, which had begun to dominate the discussion over the previous two years and was characterized by disinformation, fake news, and "alternative facts," all combining to offer a slippery understanding of what the truth actually is. Fringe movements like birtherism, which alleged that Barack Obama was born in Kenya and thus ineligible to be president and was also a Muslim planning to bring down the United States from the inside, had been growing since 2008, but the explosion of online forums like 4chan saw disinformation spreading far more quickly. The website was instrumental in circulating rumors that the Democrats were running a human-trafficking ring using restaurants as a front for pedophilia and satanic abuse, which led to a twenty-eight-year-old American man driving to Comet Ping Pong, a pizzeria in Washington, DC, and firing three shots that struck the restaurant's walls, a desk, and a door. These claims were blatantly ridiculous—worthy perhaps of a headline in one of those copies of the *National Enquirer* we occasionally see Mulder or Scully flip through when in line at the checkout counter—but Ben Lindbergh makes the point that while Tad O'Malley was conceived of before fake news became a buzzword, season eleven is "steeped in 2017, when once-disreputable and easily dismissed movements monopolized mainstream attention and staged a cultural (and Constitutional) coup."[1]

Carter says that he and the team at Ten Thirteen weren't responding to political realities in the revival seasons of the show, but it is difficult to see many of the episodes as anything other than a response to the new political climate. Season eleven's "The Lost Art of Forehead Sweat" is perhaps the most striking in this respect. Authored by Darin Morgan, who wrote two of the revival's new episodes as well as "Jose Chung's," discussed earlier in this book, the episode introduces us to Reggie Something, a conspiracy theorist and apparent former FBI agent who worked with Mulder and Scully on the X-Files. Mulder and Scully have no recollection of this, which is the point of the episode: memory is faulty and malleable, and if we can be convinced

---

1   Lindbergh. 2018. "*The X-Files* in the Post-Conspiracy Age of Trump." *The Ringer*.

what we remember isn't actually what happened, how can we be sure what the "truth" is? Much as the beginning of "Jose Chung's" sets the theme for the episode and reiterates the conceit of the show, so does the beginning of "Forehead Sweat." The episode opens with a black-and-white precredits sequence featuring a man in a late-night café telling the waiter, "I know you think I'm crazy. But it's not me, it's the world. The world's gone mad." We discover, as the camera pulls back to reveal a café that's eerily similar to the diner in "Jose Chung's" where Mulder orders piece after piece of sweet potato pie, that the man is referring to his belief that Martians are invading Earth, although the sentiment could apply to the state of the world in 2018. As the waiter tells the man that the window he thought he was looking through is actually a mirror, we see that the man is a Martian and the waiter is the Devil. After the credits, we—and Mulder—meet a man called Reggie who apparently worked with Mulder and Scully on the X-Files. Mulder has no recollection of this, and as sirens begin to sound, Reggie tells him that the first episode of *The Twilight Zone* that he thinks he ever watched—an extract of which we saw in the precredits sequence—never actually existed. The reason Mulder and Scully can't remember Reggie is that "they" are trying to erase him from society by manipulating memories.

The episode uses the Mandela effect, the misremembering of facts by multiple people, as a vehicle to consider what truth means in the current climate. Discussing the Mandela effect (which Reggie refers to as the Mengele effect), the following exchange takes place between Scully and Reggie:

> REGGIE: The Mengele effect is being intentionally orchestrated by someone.
> SCULLY: Who? And to what end?
> REGGIE: For the simple reasons that Orwell said: "He who controls the past controls the future." The ability to manipulate memory creates unlimited power. Political, economical, cultural. It runs the gamut from Holocaust denial to corporate product recognition. There are companies who are willing to pay anything, do anything, to have people forget that their products explode on impact, or suddenly catch fire. Companies

> like [the sound cuts out before Reggie can name the company] spending billions in profit to repress these memories. Only thing I haven't been able to do is figure out how they're doing it.

The capitalist uses for harnessing the Mengele effect to one side, "Forehead Sweat" highlights the problem of misremembering, or actively creating a false image of, the past in order to make political gains. I mentioned in Chapter Three the reference to past eras by both Trump and the UK's Leave EU campaign during the mid 2010s, and this recalling of "better times" proved successful. Trump was elected president, and the UK voted to leave the European Union, but both attempts to manipulate the collective memory of voters ultimately led to gains only for those already in power. The UK's decision to leave the EU has not resulted in more money being diverted to the National Health Service, which remains in crisis, and making America "great" again really meant making America white and Christian again. The positioning of "us" versus "them," which has become a common feature of this kind of political discourse, is also used by Morgan in the episode, though as is often the case when Morgan writes for the show, it is subverted.

Reggie tells Mulder that "they want you to think all conspiracies are nutty so that you ignore the ones that are true," to which Mulder responds that an omnipresent "they" is frequently heard in relation to conspiracy theories, either as a source of the theory ("They say the government are doing this") or as the force that will take action ("They are listening to you through your smart devices"). While we might accept this, drawing on our own real-world knowledge of conspiracy theorists, and believe Reggie is a conspiracy nut, we soon find out that They is actually Dr. Thaddeus Q. They, a neuroscientist who worked for NASA and discovered a way to manipulate collective memory. In an interview with *Entertainment Weekly*, Morgan stated that Trump was an inspiration for the episode, saying:

> The initial thing was trying to find some sort of Trump thing. I wanted to write something about it because [the show's]

whole premise is "The Truth is Out There," and now your fictional characters work for someone for whom the truth is a bit fuzzy. So, you should write something about that. Rather than coming up with a story idea or a plot or the weird phenomenon thing, I actually started from that viewpoint. Which is a bit different from what I've normally done.[2]

Dr. They is, in fact, clearly aligned with Trump in the episode: a voice-over introducing the character informs us, over a montage that includes They in a "Make America Great Again" baseball cap, that They was spotted at the last presidential inauguration, where "amongst the hundreds of millions who attended, he was seen occupying the last remaining seat available." With this line, Morgan brings the issue of disinformation—a growing concern in contemporary politics—front and center.

XXX

In 2012, the World Economic Forum called digital misinformation a major threat to modern society, comparable to terrorism and the failure of global governance. This was particularly evident in 2016 in the buildup to, and aftermath of, the US presidential election. Much as Cigarette Smoking Man stated that "truth is fluid and alterable" in "My Struggle III," politicians adopted the principle that truth was about not what the facts were, but what was most useful to get the desired outcome. To that end, throughout his presidential campaign, Trump painted his opponents as liars, criminals, or sufferers of mental illness but, once elected, used lies to advance his own agenda. White House Press Secretary Sean Spicer insisted the crowds at Trump's inauguration were the largest inaugural audience ever, an assertion that was easily disproved given the photographic evidence but was defended by Trump adviser Keyyanne Conway as "alternative facts." This term is clearly an oxymoron—facts by their very nature are

---

2   Coggan. 2018. "*X-Files* writer Darin Morgan teases *Twilight Zone*-inspired episode." *Entertainment Weekly*.

things that are known or proven to be true, and so you would think it is impossible to have an alternative truth when there is evidence to the contrary. But once again, *The X-Files* mirrors the real world in questioning the nature of truth.

The internet, in its infancy when *The X-Files* first aired, played a key role in this new framework, offering audiences a way to connect and talk about the show they loved, but also a space for what were previously fringe ideas to go mainstream. Growing access to the internet and easier (and cheaper) methods of communication meant these ideas were no longer limited to the small percentage of the population who could access websites; anyone could set up a website or a Facebook page and share their thoughts on everything from the moon landings to 9/11 and the dangers of vaccinations—the truth was becoming increasingly difficult to define.[3] The following exchange between Mulder and Dr. They highlights the shifting nature of belief in both the show and wider society:

> DR. THEY: Your time has passed.
> MULDER: Okay. So, what is or what was my time?
> DR. THEY: Well, it's a time when people of power thought that they could keep their secrets secret, and were willing to do anything to keep it that way. Those days are passed. Gone. We're now living in a post-cover-up, post-conspiracy age. And no doubt, the kids will come up with some catchphrase for it. PoCo or something. They'll say like, "Oh, that's so PoCo." It'll make you wish you really were dead.
> MULDER: As long as the truth gets out.
> DR. THEY: They don't really care whether the truth gets out. Because the public no longer knows what's meant by the truth.
> MULDER: What do you mean?
> DR. THEY: No one can tell the difference anymore between what's real and what's fake.
> MULDER: There's still objective truth, objective reality.

---

3   Interestingly, the first idea that William Gibson, who wrote both "Kill Switch" and "First Person Shooter," had for the show was to write an episode about "a haunted website, a page that literally kills you." But the idea was scrapped because Fox "thought not enough people knew what a website was back then. They thought it'd be confusing." (Harrison. 2015. "Can *The X-Files* exist in a post-9/11 world?" *The New Statesman*.) Showing just how much times have changed.

DR. THEY: So what?

For Dr. They and, increasingly, the world beyond *The X-Files*, objective truth is difficult to find. And even when it's found, it might not even matter. They's "so what" sums up the issues facing society on *The X-Files* return: buzzwords like "fake news" and "post-truth" had become part of a global everyday lexicon, and "the truth" was as available on Facebook and Twitter as it was in scientific journals. One of the most striking examples of this was the QAnon movement, a far-right conspiracy theory that emerged in late 2017. QAnon began with a post by a user called Q on the website 4chan, claiming to be a high-ranking US government official with access to classified government information. Among the many accusations made in a variety of posts were that a deep-state cabal including Hollywood actors, government officials, and politicians was involved in child sex trafficking and that it was working against Trump during his time in office. That QAnon circulated online is, perhaps, no surprise, and the internet plays a key part in how Dr. They shapes people's collective memories. He is a purveyor of "phony fake news," a "presentation of real facts, but in a way that assures no one will believe any of it." This is rather different from disinformation in the real world, which presents false information in a way that assures people that what they are reading is the truth, but this comment on the nature of truth is at the heart of both the episode and Morgan's response to real-world events. The following exchange between Mulder and Dr. They explicitly links the conspiracy theory at the heart of the episode, the government, and online disinformation:

> DR. THEY: Well, in the old days, I would never have come out and admitted to you yes, I can change people's collective memories. The point is I can tell you all of this right out in the open because it doesn't matter who knows about it. They won't know whether to believe it or not.
> MULDER: To be honest, I'm not believing any of this.
> DR. THEY: Believe what you want to believe. That's what everybody does nowadays anyway. You're only proving my point, you twit. But, full disclosure, you're

right. I can't control people's minds. Although, it turns
out, you don't really have to. All you need is some
people to think it's possible. And then you've sown the
seeds of uncertainty. All you really need is a laptop.
MULDER: So that's what this has all been about? The
spread of online disinformation?

The spread of fake news and disinformation throughout the course of
the Brexit referendum and the Trump presidential campaign, as well
as the rise of QAnon, demonstrates just how easy it is to obscure the
truth.

XXX

There are several more explicit references to Trump during this episode.
Dr. They tells Mulder that "our current president once said something
truly profound. He said, 'Nobody knows for sure,'" and the retelling
of Reggie, Mulder, and Scully's final case draws directly from a speech
Trump gave in June 2015. In the episode, Mulder, Scully, and Reggie
meet an alien representative of the Intergalactic Union of Sentient
Beings from All Known Universes and Beyond. The alien tells them
that they are barring humans from exploring the galaxy by "building
a wall," then adds:

It will be a beautiful, albeit invisible, electromagnetic
wall that will subatomically incinerate any probes
you attempt to send beyond your solar system. [. . .
] We can't allow your kind to infiltrate the rest of the
cosmos. You're not sending us your best people. You're
bringing drugs, you're bringing crime, you're bringing
rapists. And some, I assume, are good people. But we
have no choice, believe me.

The wall of course refers to the wall Trump announced he would build
across the southern US border to prevent Mexicans from entering
the country. Morgan says he never hesitated to inject too much of
the political climate into the episode, adding, "I thought, *People who
support Trump or who support the wall, what would they think if an*

alien came down and flipped it on them? How would they regard it?[4] For many fans, the episode was one of the standouts for the season.

The year that *The X-Files* returned to our screens was the same year that Oxford Dictionaries selected "post-truth' as its word of the year, defining it as shorthand for "circumstances in which objective facts are less influential in shaping public opinion than appeals to emotion and personal belief."[5] While Carter, addressing the connections between *The X-Files* and emerging conspiracy movements during promotion for *Fight the Future*, argued that "the series is neither about paramilitary groups nor does it propose revolutionary tactics. It only suggests to the audience to question authority and not to trust any institution,"[6] it did tap into a specific kind of conspiratorial thinking that became commonplace in the twenty-first century, bolstered by fake news and the appeal to emotion over logic. This came to a head with the attacks on the US Capitol building by Trump supporters on January 6, 2021, following his defeat in the 2020 presidential election. Trump had claimed that the election had been "stolen by emboldened radical-left Democrats"[7] with rumors circulating that voters had been forced to use felt-tipped pens that scanners couldn't read. Claims about voter fraud, deep-state manipulation of voting machines, and the failure of the "lamestream" media to report the truth that Trump had actually won the election appealed to the emotions of Trump supporters who believed that they were standing up for justice. The fact that none of these things had happened didn't matter, and despite the truth being reported by the media, Trump fans continued to believe his story: as Dr. They says, no one knows anymore what's real and what's fake.

This privileging of feeling over fact in contemporary politics does, in some ways, mirror the fundamental tension at the heart of *The X-Files*. Scully's belief in science clashes with Mulder's faith in personal

---

4   Coggan. 2018b. "*X-Files* writer breaks down his Trump-inspired episode 'about truth and lying.'" *Entertainment Weekly*.

5   BBC. 2016. "'Post-truth' declared word of the year by Oxford Dictionaries."

6   Der Spiegel. 1998. "Achtung, Verschwörer!" *Eat The Corn*.

7   Naylor. 2021. "Read Trump's Jan. 6 Speech, A Key Part Of Impeachment Trial." *National Public Radio*.

experience; while Scully reaches conclusions on what she believes is the truth based on fact, Mulder relies on leaps of faith and what *feels* right. Carter said in a 2016 interview:

> It's funny because I've always said it's Scully's show. If it weren't for the science, Mulder would just be another crazy out there, tilting at windmills. So while I believe Mulder's anti-authority, anti-government bent is certainly the thing that narrowly always wins the day, it is Scully's rationalism that is absolutely important to what the show is.[8]

In the post-truth era, however, science is treated with skepticism, and Scully's rationality seems to be in the minority. As Carter said in an interview with *TV Insider*, "Fake news, science being thrown out the window, conspiracies—these things that are causing huge shifts in culture, politics and, in many cases, morality right now will play into the new stories we tell."[9] The engagement with contemporary politics across both revival seasons was controversial for some fans, one writing "much of what worked in the original now feels dated and [Carter's] vision of the series was oftentimes stretching to make itself feel relevant and politically engaged with its too obvious digs at the Trump administration," but Morgan argues that using the contemporary political climate allowed him to make a comment about perspectives on truth and lies in a way that wouldn't turn people off. One fan, responding to a questionnaire I released after the season ended, wrote, "The best part of season 11 was [Chris Carter] taking on the current state of affairs--fake governments, fake news, the brainwashing of the media, the role of technology." *The X-Files* was heavily influenced by cultural events in the US and steeped in the paranoia that was prevalent in popular discourse, and so dealing with concepts like fake news, misinformation, and truther conspiracy

---

8   Saxelby. 2016. "*The X-Files* Creator Explains How The Show Knew Everything About The Future." *Fader.*

9   Roffman. 2017. "Inside *The X-Files* Season 11: Mulder and Scully Take on Their Biggest Mystery Yet." *TV Insider.*

theories in the revival seasons was par for the course. Yet seasons ten and eleven tapped into the post-truth moment that had begun in the early part of the twenty-first century so successfully that they appeared to predict events that would happen years later.

SECTION THREE

I WANT TO BELIEVE

CHAPTER 7

Subverting Gender Expectations On and Off the Screen

"Eight million years out of Africa."
"Look who's holding the door."
—Mulder and Scully ("The Jersey Devil")

The X-Files has been lauded for its depiction of a strong female character, and the gender reversal of Mulder (the male believer) and Scully (the female skeptic) has been one of the most discussed features of the series. Chris Carter has on many occasions talked about the conscious decision to reverse the gender roles of the show's protagonists, saying in his introduction to the 1996 "Pilot/Deep Throat" VHS, "I wanted to flip the gender types, the stereotypes that we have. I wanted Mulder, the male, to be the believer, the intuitor, and I wanted Scully to be the skeptic, the one which is usually the traditional male role." In a 1997 interview with *Rolling Stone* magazine, he said, "The two characters I came up with sort of represented those two sides of myself: the scientific and the intuitive. Then I switched

THE TRUTH IS STILL OUT THERE

genders."[1] These assertions are reinforced by other members of the production team, for example Frank Spotnitz's response to a BBC Cult interview:

> I think the first thing, the most obvious thing, to say about their relationship is it's a Yin and Yang. It's the believer and the skeptic. Yet it's flipped from the beginning because the woman is the skeptic and the man is the believer. That is a clear switch on gender stereotypes. The man has the more emotional, intuitive position and the woman's got the more cold, rational approach. That immediately made it interesting. Then they're both fiercely intelligent, very smart and very interesting.[2]

While it wasn't entirely unheard for women to take the lead role or to be seen as strong female characters (Carter has called *Silence of the Lambs* an inspiration, saying, "It's not a mistake that Dana Scully has red hair like Clarice Starling"[3]), it was still unusual enough that the press, fans, and academics pointed it out as a defining feature of the show. Television, especially in the eighties, had seen the marginalization of lead female characters in prime time shows, replaced by stories that focused on women's role within the family as homemaker and caregiver. Where shows existed with male and female coleads, the man's point of view was the authoritative one—and the series often ended up with the pair in a relationship. A refreshing change—at least in the first few seasons—was that Mulder and Scully's relationship was platonic, built on layers of trust and intimacy but with no fear that the two of them jumping into bed together would ruin the show, as had happened with *Moonlighting*. Scully is also equal in intelligence to Mulder. He might be an Oxford-educated psychologist, but she is a scientist who rewrote Einstein as an undergraduate and was recruited into the FBI straight out of medical school.

---

1   Lipsky 1997.

2   BBC Online. 2000. "Cult–*X Files*–Frank Spotnitz interview."

3   Rhodes 2008.

It's obvious to fans that Gillian Anderson is a perfect fit for Scully, and it was obvious to Carter when he saw her audition, as he relates in the VHS introduction: "She came in and read the part with a seriousness and intensity that I knew the Scully character had to have and I knew she was the right person for the part." Fox had other ideas, though. Anderson was a relative unknown to the network, having done little TV work, and they also wanted Scully to be played by someone who would fit their prime time formula, meaning, in Anderson's own words, "bustier" and "leggier." She revealed that the network had a different Anderson in mind: *Baywatch* star Pamela Anderson, who was "more familiar to them in terms of what was on TV at the time. They were looking for someone bustier, taller, leggier than me. They couldn't fathom how David and me could equal success."[4] Carter held firm, staking both the pilot and his career on Anderson, and the character, and the actress, rose to success. She plays Scully with the seriousness that was required for a scientist, but her intelligence and compassion also shine through. In doing background reading for this book, I picked up Sherrie A. Innes's *Tough Girls: Women Warriors and Wonder Women in Popular Culture* and found this quote really interesting: "I am particularly interested in the depiction of Scully because she frequently is overshadowed by Mulder. Moreover, the actor David Duchovny is far more the focal point of the show than Anderson."[5] I must admit I'm not entirely convinced by this. It might be hindsight, of course—some twenty plus years later I hear far more from fans about Gillian Anderson than I do about David Duchovny, and Scully is discussed, analyzed, and referred to far more than Mulder is (as much I do love Mulder). There are certainly points in the series where Scully is overruled by Mulder, but I wouldn't say she's overshadowed. The fact that she's the point of view through which audiences see and understand the show (as I talked about in earlier chapters) makes her a pretty significant element of the series. But let's take a look at Mulder and what he can tell us about gender in the late twentieth century.

---

4   Reynolds. 2008. "Pamela Anderson 'nearly cast as Scully'." *Digital Spy*.

5   Inness. 1999. *Tough Girls: Women Warriors and Wonder Women in Popular Culture*. University of Pennsylvania Press, p. 95.

<u>XXX</u>

Mulder is not your everyman—he is an Oxford-educated psychologist who graduated with honors from the Quantico FBI training academy and was a young star in the behavioral science unit. He runs his own division and is clearly an authority on the X-Files, looked up to by others (albeit within the UFO community rather than more mainstream sectors). He is also stereotypically attractive, follows the all-American sport of baseball, and plays basketball. All of these mark him as successful model of traditional masculinity—as the blockhead points out in "Humbug," as we cut to Mulder standing hands on hips, one foot up on the steps of a trailer and looking into the distance, "I've seen the future, and the future looks just like him." Yet despite all of this, he is also undeniably a bit weird, "spooky," as his colleagues refer to him. His interests lie in the "other," driven of course by his sister's abduction. Women are often used as plot devices to further a male character's storyline or character development—think Liam Neeson's character in *Taken*, who has to track down his kidnapped daughter, or the execution of William Wallace's wife, which sparks his rebellion in *Braveheart*. Samantha's abduction is the driving force of the series and remains at its heart, and we see frequent references to her, as well as episodes in which she appears on screen both as a child and an adult ("Colony"). What Samantha's abduction allows us, though, is a far more emotionally available, and vulnerable, Mulder.

In this respect, Mulder reflects changing attitudes toward masculinity in the 1990s, in contrast to the conservative, hyper-masculinity of previous eras. Carter deftly shows this division between Mulder and the older, patriarchal figures of *The X-Files*. Mulder's own relationship with his father is strained, something we see in season one's "Roland" when Mulder recounts a dream: "I dreamt I was swimming in this pool, and I could see my father underwater, but when I dove down, the water stung my eyes. And there was another man in the pool. He was watching me. He upset me. He was asking me questions I didn't want to answer. I tried to leave, but I couldn't find my father." Bill Mulder's absence throughout Mulder's childhood extends into adulthood and undeniably shapes Mulder, even down to his habit of eating sunflower seeds. In season two's "Aubrey," he tells Scully about a memory of waking from nightmares of being abandoned as a child to hear the sound of his father eating sunflower seeds in his study. Rather than becoming cold and aloof like his father, though—in "Colony," Bill Mulder evades a handshake when Mulder arrives at his house—he embraces this vulnerability and turns it from a weakness into a strength. The scene of Mulder returning to his apartment in "One Breath," sinking to the floor and crying, is highly emotionally charged and gives me goosebumps every time I see it. It demonstrates just how important Scully is to Mulder not just professionally—she's the sounding board for his more outlandish leaps of faith—but also personally. Mulder offers emotional support to Scully when her father dies, for example, but he also accepts the support she offers him. In the fourth season's "Paper Hearts," Mulder is woken by a dream in which he finds the body of a young girl, a victim of serial killer John Lee Roche. Mulder, beginning to suspect the killer was also responsible for abducting his sister, visits Roche in prison, and he subsequently arranges for his release in order to travel to Martha's Vineyard and discover the truth about Samantha's disappearance. Ultimately, Mulder is forced to shoot Roche after he absconds with his FBI badge and gun and abducts another girl. The episode ends with Mulder sitting in his office, staring disconsolately at his desk. "Why don't you go home and get some sleep?" Scully asks, before Mulder pulls her into an embrace. Mulder's decision to speak to Roche in the episode comes from a dream, and this reliance on intuition, hunches, and "gut feelings" is another way Mulder flips the gender switch. Academic Joe Bellon sees Mulder as a rebel against traditional masculinity, writing:

> For his part, Mulder no more signifies the traditional male cop than Scully signifies the traditional female. He is prone to strange moods, strong emotions, and light-hearted comments. Unlike more traditional male cop characters who flaunt a devil-may-care attitude as a kind of macho display, however, Mulder represents the emotional and empathic balance to Scully's logic and rationality. He cried over the abduction of

his sister when he was a child ("Conduit"), he empathizes with families who lose children, and he is obsessed with truth.[6]

All of this is in stark contrast to the older, patriarchal figures of *The X-Files*. Unlike Cigarette Smoking Man, Deep Throat, and even his father, all of whom have killed with impunity, kept secrets from the people closest to them, and fundamentally altered the course of humanity for their own ends, Mulder is open to new experiences—the blessing way ritual in season three's opening episode aligns him with the Navajo people and a spirituality beyond the white Christianity of the majority of Americans, including Scully. Mulder is spiritual, not religious, in tune with the psyche and in many ways a polar opposite to Scully. But neither can work without the other.

Scully is highly regarded by her male colleagues, giving us a contemporary women not only surviving but thriving in a male-dominated workplace. She's coolly rational, she can wield a gun with the best of them and isn't afraid to speak her mind whatever the consequences. We see evidence of how capable and respected Scully is early on, in the first three episodes of season one. She performs an autopsy in the pilot, rescues Mulder from Ellens Air Base in "Deep Throat," and is contacted by a fellow agent because of her expertise in "Squeeze." But I think it's "Jersey Devil" where we first really see the show's concerns around gender coming out. The episode is one of the few to show Scully in a social setting beyond the X-Files. Attending a children's birthday party, Scully converses with her friend Ellen about whether she wants to have children and whether Mulder would make a suitable romantic partner. He wouldn't—he's obsessed with his work, as evidenced by the fact that he calls Scully to collect him from jail, where he's ended up while looking for evidence of the Jersey Devil. Scully refuses to stay in Atlantic City with Mulder, though, telling him she has a date and that unlike him, she'd like to have a life. The date seems fine, though to viewers, Scully's attention appears to be elsewhere, and when Mulder calls, she answers. Fans who want

6   Bellon 1999, p. 150.

to see a relationship between Mulder and Scully (I am not in this category) might see this as evidence but I don't think it is. What we see is actually quite a subversive statement on Scully's part for the early nineties: she chooses her career. We know that her date is interested in Scully and wants to see her again; we know he assumes she wants children (even though she tells Ellen she doesn't know if she's cut out for that). In an era when it was still common for women to stay at home and look after the children while the husband went out to work, Scully making that decision is really important. The nineties marked a change from the more conservative, Reagan-era eighties, and this interaction between Mulder and Scully at the end of the episode sums that up:

> MULDER: Who was that on the phone?
> SCULLY: A guy.
> MULDER: A guy. Same guy as the guy you had dinner with the other night?
> SCULLY: Same guy.
> MULDER: You gonna have dinner with him again?
> SCULLY: I don't think so.
> MULDER: No interest?
> SCULLY: Not at this time.
> MULDER: What are you doing?
> SCULLY: I'm going with you to the Smithsonian.
> MULDER: Don't you have a life, Scully?
> SCULLY: Keep that up, Mulder, and I'll hurt you like that beast woman.
> MULDER: Eight million years out of Africa.
> SCULLY: Look who's holding the door.

I love this scene not just because I can repeat it word for word, but because it shows times are changing. Scully is the one holding the door open for Mulder, not the other way around. And while that might seem like a small thing, it sets the tone for the series, and the rest of the decade. This is a time when women are breaking into male-dominated workplaces, a fact highlighted in season two's "Soft Light" when Scully is asked to help a former student, Detective Kelly Ryan. Although women are becoming more visible in law enforcement, they aren't common as investigators in the field, and when Detective Ryan is under pressure from her male colleagues to solve the case, Scully not only supports her but also tells Mulder she knows the position she's in: "She's a woman trying to survive the boys' club, Mulder. Believe me, I know how she feels." It's also a time when women can choose not to have children or stay at home and be mothers. And while this is a choice that Scully could make herself, we never really get to know for sure—the Syndicate, and Carter—take that choice away from her.

XXX

I have been pretty complimentary toward Scully and the show's broader reflection of gender so far, but I can't deny that there were some less than positive aspects too. A lot of academic analysis tends to focus on these in terms of feminism, a new form of which was emerging in the nineties. In the UK, when I was a teenager, this manifested itself as "girl power" with pop groups like the Spice Girls promoting the importance of loyalty among women, self-belief, and individualism. While these are of course important, they did clash at times with second-wave feminism, which had focused on gaining equal rights for women, and third-wave feminism, which stressed the importance of understanding the experiences of women beyond the middle-class, educated, white women who had benefited most during the second wave. *The X-Files* rarely addressed these wider issues. Scholar Emily Regan-Wills argues:

> Scully speaks vaguely of the tensions between career and motherhood, makes reference to herself as a "woman in a man's world," and occasionally deals with discrimination from other law enforcement officials. But she simply soldiers on, assuming that by behaving in as unimpeachable a manner as possible, she will be able to personally triumph over the sexism she experiences.[7]

---

7   Regan-Wills. 2013. "Fannish discourse communities and the construction of gender in *The X-Files.*" *Transformative Works and Cultures.*

And she has a point. Episodes that involve Scully interacting with female law enforcement agents who are similarly "women in a man's world" portray them as competitors for Mulder's affection. When we meet Phoebe Green in "Fire," there's immediate tension between her and Scully, with Phoebe whispering "She hates me" to Mulder after they've been introduced. In "Syzygy," Scully is uncharacteristically sharp with, and catty about, Detective White. Being charitable, I think we can see both of these as attempts to show that Mulder and Scully's relationship is special because it doesn't fall into the trap of developing into a romantic relationship, but I think that reasoning falls a bit short. What we see instead is the trope that women cannot work together because they're competing for the same man (which raises its head again in season six with the introduction of the woman fans love to hate, Diana Fowley). What we also get, though, are a fair few episodes where Scully is portrayed as weak and powerless. Regan Wills gives three examples of how this happens in the narrative: "Scully as abductee, as sexually desirable, and as a (potential) mother."[8] The first of these wasn't an intentional part of the mytharc: Anderson announced she was pregnant after season one, and Fox wanted her role to be recast. Rather than do that, Carter decided to have Scully abducted by aliens, which Frank Spotnitz describes as "the best thing that ever happened to the series."[9] I'm not entirely convinced of that, but what I think is really interesting in terms of the girl power of the nineties and the debates that raised about women's bodies is Regan Wills's second example.

Despite fans' love for Scully, and Gillian Anderson—who was voted *FHM*'s sexiest woman of the year in 1996 and was often referred to as the "thinking man's crumpet"— Scully is rarely depicted as sexual. In the first few seasons of the show, her appearance isn't particularly feminine: she wears pantsuits and little makeup, and her hair is unstyled. Even the outfit she wears on her date in "Jersey Devil" (a white lace top and black slacks) screams eighties mom. Femininity

8   Ibid.

9   Hurwitz and Knowles 2008, p. 44.

isn't an important part of Scully's character, until it serves the plot. When Scully is seen as feminine, as sexual, things start going wrong. In "Gender Bender," Brother Andrew's attraction to Scully almost leads to her being killed, and despite the fact that members of the Kindred are able to manipulate their victims into performing activities they might not want to perform, Mulder blames Scully for putting herself in that position, saying, "I know what I saw, Scully. And I saw you about to do the wild thing with some stranger." This is a theme that unfortunately continues throughout the show. Season four's "Never Again," which features Scully demanding to know why she doesn't have a desk even after working with Mulder for four years, places her in what Linda Badley calls the "Scully-almost-seduced" and "Scully-in-peril" combination.[10] With Mulder in Graceland (because where else would he go on enforced leave), Scully heads to Philadelphia to follow up on a case. Tracking an informant to a tattoo parlor, she meets Ed Jerse, recipient of a murderous, talkative tattoo, who invites her to dinner. Ed's tattoo, voiced by Jodie Foster (another *Silence of the Lambs* connection), is not happy with their mutual attraction, and Ed ultimately attacks Scully after they have spent the night together. When Scully returns to the office after being released from the hospital, Mulder asks, "All this because I didn't get you a desk?" Scully responds, "Not everything is about you, Mulder. This is my life." But as we'll see in the next couple of chapters, that isn't entirely the case.

XXX

It's easy in hindsight to look back at the first few seasons of the show and see the problems associated with the representation of gender. These were representative of the wider culture, both in the TV industry and beyond. When the show first aired, Anderson was paid less than Duchovny. While Duchovny was the better known star, having appeared in *Twin Peaks* as well as several films, that Anderson

---

10   Badley. 2000. "Scully Hits the Glass Ceiling: Postmodernism, Postfeminism, Posthumanism, and *The X-Files*." In Elyce Rae Helford (ed) *Fantasy Girls: Gender in the New Universe of Science Fiction and Fantasy Television*. Rowman & Littlefield, p. 72.

earned less for several seasons—despite how integral a part of the show Scully was and how talented an actress Anderson was (and still is)—is mind-boggling and shows how important the fight for equal pay is. Not only that, but Anderson has since revealed that she had to stand several feet behind Duchovny on camera:

> I can only imagine that at the beginning, they wanted me to be the sidekick, or that, somehow, maybe it was enough of a change just to see a woman having this kind of intellectual repartee with a man on camera, and surely the audience couldn't deal with actually seeing them walk side by side![11]

To fans of the show, this is clearly ridiculous; there is no *X-Files* without Mulder and Scully (a contentious topic for the final three seasons), but Anderson pushed both for equal pay and for being seen as an equal on-screen. She also became an off-screen role model, becoming a spokesperson for the Feminist Majority Foundation in 1996. Given attitudes toward gender at the time, what Anderson and Carter did was pretty revolutionary and helped pave the way for changing representations of gender in television. We may not have seen characters like *Fringe*'s Olivia Dunham or *Bones*'s Doctor Temperance Brennan without Scully, and we'd quite possibly have fewer women working in science, technology, engineering, or medicine—as we'll see in the next chapter.

---

11   Brech. 2017. "Gillian Anderson takes aim at *The X-Files*' lack of gender diversity." *Stylist*.

CHAPTER 8

Gender Beyond the Show: Fan Fiction and the Scully Effect

"Woman, get back in here and make me a sandwich!"
– Mulder ("Arcadia")

So far, I've talked about Mulder and Scully and their depictions on the show and how the character of Scully paved the way for more increased representation of women on screen and in the lives of women in the real world. In this chapter, I want to carry on looking at how female fans responded to these portrayals of gender, but I'm going to do it a bit differently. I'll come back to the "Scully effect"—the impact Scully had on encouraging women to enter STEM fields—later, but first I want to go back to my early days as an academic and a fan of the show. Now, I love Scully. I think she's an awesome character who made real strides in terms of the way women are represented on television. But—and I may have mentioned this a couple of times already—I was not a shipper. I never wanted Mulder and Scully to get involved, and while I loved the unresolved sexual tension between them, I thought that pairing them romantically would ruin the series (I still maintain this, and I know what happened in *I Want to Believe* and the revival seasons). So when one Diana Fowley appeared on the scene, I thought nothing of it. *The X-Files* already had some major female secondary characters in the form of Samantha and Teena Mulder, Cassandra Spencer, and Marita Covarrubias, so the inclusion of another one was no big deal. Or so I thought . . .

Fowley was introduced in the season five finale, "The End," and at the beginning of season six was working on the X-Files with Jeffrey Spender after Mulder was removed from his post. Although Fowley's motives remained ambiguous throughout the course of her time on the series, she appeared to be working closely with Cigarette Smoking Man, and many viewers assumed she was associated with the Syndicate and so working against Mulder and Scully in their pursuit of the truth. Now that would be a fair reason for fans to hate her; it's one reason they love to hate Krycek (or "Rat Boy") so much. But that wasn't the reason. Carter has said that Fowley "was a character you were destined to hate because she was a competitor for Mulder's affection with Scully,"[1] and hate people did. *Den of Geek* ranked Fowley among its ten most disappointing female characters in sci-fi TV, while a slew of hate groups sprung up after her introduction to the series. The Diana Fowley Hater's Brigade was created in 1999 and contained links to fan fiction, poems, and songs about Fowley (almost all of them wishing her dead) as well as a mailing list. The Anti Diana Fowley Archive, also set up in 1999, listed fan fiction relating to Fowley and included titles such as "Die Fowley Die!" and "Diana Fowley Dies!!!" Fan art featuring photo manipulations of Fowley as a witch or demon and memes ("Fowley by name, Fowl by nature") also circulated in the fandom. In their analysis of *The X-Files* fan fiction, Christine Scodari and Jenna L. Felder suggest that the trust Mulder puts into Fowley and his refusal to clarify his relationship with her to Scully caused what shippers viewed as a breach in the partnership (and the developing romance between the two leads). They write that "Fan fic answers sixth season chagrin by stating in headers that the

---

1   Hurwitz and Knowles 2008, p. 131.

objectionable events are going to be ignored, or by reconciling the agents and eliminating 'The Fowl One,' often mortally and at Mulder or Scully's hand."[2] I found—and continue to find—this fascinating. I talked a bit in the last chapter about the trope of women seeing each other as competitors for a man's affections, and seasons six and seven went to town on that. Mulder and Fowley make repeated eye contact while Scully sits in the passenger seat, a third wheel; Scully has to find out from the Lone Gunmen that Fowley was Mulder's "chickadee" and even asks them to find out why the two split up; and the confrontation between Scully and Fowley in "Amor Fati" clearly shows the animosity between the two.

XXX

Thinking back to waves of feminism, the animosity between Scully and Fowley was a symptom of the way postfeminist popular culture positioned women in opposition to, or in competition with, each other. It was also, as some have argued, a lazy way for Carter to introduce some tension into a season. As one fan said, "Chris has droned on and on about his objections to "soapy" plot devices yet he goes right ahead and uses the soapiest idea of all: the meddling ex-girlfriend that returns from abroad."[3] I've always thought that Scully and Fowley are more similar than they appear, though—they both care about Mulder, but they're also both female FBI special agents working within the male-dominated field of law enforcement, and both were treated pretty badly by the show's writers at times. In fan fiction about episodes in which Scully is depicted as more feminine (and therefore weaker), writers find ways to critique that association. Scholar Emily Regan-Wills argues that the negative association between sexuality and autonomy in canon rarely bleeds into fan fiction. Instead, "The Dana Scully who appears in sexually explicit fic is assertive, confidant

---

2   Scodari, and Felder. 2000. "Creating a pocket universe: 'Shippers,' fan fiction, and *The X-Files* Online." *Communication Studies*, 51 (3), p. 247.

3   Ibid p. 248.

[sic], and powerfully in control both of her sexuality and her life"[4]—unlike in the episodes these stories are based on. What I always found interesting was that while fans would turn to fan fiction to address some of the wrongs they felt had been done to Scully, they didn't do the same with Fowley. Or at least most of them didn't.

I began writing fan fiction about *The X-Files* when one of my secondary school English teachers gave us a writing prompt using the show. That first story is now long gone, thankfully. But I was hooked, and as soon as we got the internet at home, I joined the BBC Cult messageboards to share stories with other fans. I kept this up even while the show was off air, joining the popular platform LiveJournal, where I met scores of other fans, including some who liked Fowley. Discussions about the character were contentious—this was the internet, after all—but I found writers who were intrigued by her lack of development on the show. As one wrote:

> Diana Fowley is one of the most neglected, misunderstood, and hated characters in TXF fandom. It's no secret that I love her. I'm not writing a defense of her character (or her casting) because I suspect those of you who don't like Diana wouldn't read it anyway, and those of you who do, don't need it. But I will tell you why I like writing and reading fic about her: (1.) she's an intelligent, complicated, middle-aged woman with divided loyalties, and (2.) smart as she is, she's still in love with someone she knows she can't have.[5]

Through fan fiction, fans got to explore Fowley's motivations and come to understand the character. It is this barely hinted-at vulnerability that I find interesting as both a writer and a reader. As much as fans might complain about Carter's tendency to leave loose ends, these plot holes allowed us to create a backstory for Fowley that offered a more sympathetic and three-dimensional character than the one we

---

4   Regan-Wills 2013.

5   Jones. 2013b. "Mulder/Scully versus the G-Woman and the Fowl One" in Anne Jamison (ed) *Fic: Why Fanfiction Is Taking Over the World*, Smart Pop p. 119.

see on-screen. The wedding ring Mulder wears in a flashback in the season six episode "Unusual Suspects" hints at a previous relationship, and I (along with other fans) have taken that to mean he was married to Fowley. But what would such a relationship have looked like? And why did it go so horribly wrong? In my own personal canon, Fowley was sent to seduce Mulder in order for the Syndicate to keep tabs on him. Neither she nor Cigarette Smoking Man had any idea she'd fall in love with him, but as she does, her loyalties become more and more divided—explaining both why she was sent overseas and why she sacrificed herself to save Mulder's life in season seven's "The Sixth Extinction II: Amor Fati." This sacrifice also has the function of making Fowley both more sympathetic and more traditionally feminine, as she is aligned with the other women of *The X-Files* who have made sacrifices for, or been sacrificed by, the men in their lives. Fan fiction becomes an important tool that fans use to critique constructions of gender on the show. By drawing on their knowledge of the series to fill out stories with detail, fan fiction writers are able to subvert the clichés and stereotypes evident in the series, making Fowley a stronger and more three-dimensional character than depicted on *The X-Files*. In fan fiction, she's no longer the "soapy" plot device; rather, she becomes a means through which fans can comment on male writers' depictions of ex-girlfriends, competitors for male affection, and post-feminist women whose enemies are no longer men, but other women.

What fan fiction also does that the series isn't great at doing is show more than just heterosexual relationships. There are almost no gay or lesbian characters in *The X-Files* (there are no transgender characters with the possible exception of "Gender Bender", but that's debatable and pretty problematic in the context of the episode). Although gay and lesbian characters on television weren't common at the time, the nineties had given us a lesbian wedding on *Friends*, the coming out of Ellen Morgan on *Ellen*, and Ellen DeGeneres's real-life coming out on *The Oprah Winfrey Show*. Considering how much *The X-Files* did to counter stereotypes around gender, it's frustrating that the first time we see openly gay characters on the series is in season seven's "X-Cops" (a lesbian couple does appear in "all things" a few episodes later and share a kiss on screen, but they are not the focus of the episode).

The episode features Steve and Edy, a gay couple who witnessed an attack and who Mulder thinks might also be targeted. The depiction of Steve and Edy is, unfortunately, a clichéd one. When the police knock on their door with camera crew at hand, Edy's response is to run off camera and change into a turban and brightly colored robe, telling the crew on his return, "I'm ready for my close-up." This depiction plays into the stereotype of gay men as melodramatic, and it doesn't age well. Despite the clichés, though, the episode doesn't treat the characters maliciously. They survive the episode, Edy is assured that Steve isn't going to leave him, and they are shown as clearly in love. While they are stereotypes, they are also, as Sergeant Duthie says, "good folks." The introduction of Monica Reyes in season eight gave some fans hope that we would see a queer character in a prime position on the show—certainly fans have argued that Reyes is in love with Scully, especially following the scene where Scully is in labor and Reyes tells her she looks "amazingly beautiful." The show's producers did apparently consider it, but in an interview with *TV Guide*, John Shiban said they ultimately ruled out making Reyes a lesbian, saying "It's the kind of baggage that we didn't want to deal with this kind of character right now. We had other ideas that we were more excited about."[6] This was disappointing for both the show and its fans, but this is where fan fiction comes in again.

Henry Jenkins, an expert in studying fandom, argues that fan fiction is a form of resistance where fans "actively assert their mastery over the mass-produced texts."[7] If the writers and producers weren't going to give fans same-sex relationships in the show, then the fans simply went ahead and did it themselves. A surprising number of fans wrote fan fiction putting Scully and Fowley in a romantic relationship. Although I'm sure many fans would balk at that, given their hatred of Fowley, it does allow writers to explore issues around gender and power that we don't really see in the show. idella's *The Future's So Bright I Gotta Wear Shades* shows Scully and Fowley developing a relationship following

---

6   Ausiello. 2001. "*X-Files*'s Lesbian Shocker." *TV Guide*.

7   Jenkins. 1992. *Textual Poachers: Television, Fans and Participatory Culture*. Routledge, p. 23.

Mulder's disappearance after being reinstated to *The X-Files* in season six.[8] The story is made of five parts and begins in the way viewers of the series would expect it to following Fowley's apparent betrayal of Mulder at the end of season five. Scully is partnered with Fowley and is suspicious of her motivations—so far mirroring viewers' (and readers') assumptions: Fowley is not to be trusted, and her assignment to the X-Files as Scully's partner is further evidence of her role as spy. As the story progresses, though, Scully's (and thus the reader's) attitude to Fowley shifts. At one point, Scully notices that Fowley is quieter than usual and wonders if it's because of the remarks made by the (male) law enforcement officers they had encountered. Her concern and compassion for the other woman is evident: "What could she say that Fowley doesn't already know? Fowley could spout the same platitudes at her. Scully slows down for a red light. 'Small towns, you know,' she says. 'Small minds.'" We also see fan fiction that puts Scully and Reyes in a relationship as well as Mulder and Krycek—a very popular pairing. In this way, just as the show pushed some of the boundaries around gender representation, so do fans. Taking the bare bones of relationships that were hinted at in the show's subtext and writing stories that explore them in more details enables fans to not only play with expectations around gender and sexuality, but also to move the show from television into other participatory spaces. It wasn't just through writing fan fiction that fans could address gender, though. Thanks to the way Scully was portrayed on the show, fans were inspired to enter the fields of science, technology, engineering, and mathematics and make a real-world impact in these areas.

XXX

Scully was the first female scientist many fans had seen portrayed on prime time television, and during a time when young girls in particular were being told they could be anything they wanted to be, she became an inspiration. Gina Rumbaugh points out that "women

---

8   idella. 2010. *The Future's So Bright I Gotta Wear Shades*. Livejournal.

identify with Scully as a contemporary woman who faces challenges and doubts and who endeavors to achieve a fulfilling life. It is on this fundamental level of human experience that Scully is best understood as a role model."[9] Anderson has also talked about the impact Scully had on both fans and on herself:

> There was a time when I started reading the letters and people were saying, "You saved my life," or interviewers would say that Scully was a role model for young women. It stroked my ego for about five minutes before I thought, I don't know if I can handle this. I always felt that they were talking about Scully; it had nothing to do with me. But the more I started to talk about her character traits – how honest she was, how passionate about doing the right thing – the more I took cues from the way she handled herself.[10]

Scully, and by extension Anderson, is cited as a role model by many *X-Files* fans. One, who was bullied as a child, says it was through Scully that she found someone she could aspire to be like:

> Dana Scully to me is the perfect role model. An intelligent woman, working every day in a typically "man's" world – she's worked damned hard to be where she is and she's someone who every young woman should aspire to be like. Strong, determined, faithful, relentless, caring.[11]

This fan went on to create a fan group that undertook charity work inspired by Anderson. Honesty, dedication, strength, and loyalty are attributes given to Scully, and Anderson, by fans. These characteristics are important to fans, and as a result they model themselves on the

---

9   Rumbaugh. 2008. *X-chromosomes within The X-Files: An Examination of Celebrity Role Models Agent Scully and Gillian Anderson*. VDM Verlag Dr. Muller Aktiengesellschaft & Co. KG, p. 57.

10   Flaherty. 2002. "Case Closed." *Entertainment Weekly*.

11   Jones 2012.

character. Another fan told me:

> I basically fell so in love with Scully that I wanted to be like her however I could. Initially, I thought "maybe I should act!" but I realized that it wasn't acting like Scully or even being Gillian that I wanted...but being like Scully, the character herself. I now work for the government in humanitarian aid but it was the initial idea of Scully that snowballed into getting me here. I also can't help but assume that in 12+ years, I've also begun to embody some of the traits/influences of Scully, which could possibly translate into fuelling this "save the world" complex I've got. I'm sure it would still be there, regardless, but who knows what I would be up to without *X-Files*. Scully made it ok to feel different from others and I kind of just embraced and ran with it.[12]

Although some people might mock the idea of taking attributes from a beloved character and implementing them in your daily life, this actually shows how important role models like Scully can be. We make deep connections with the characters we see on TV or in films or read about in books, and it's no surprise that young girls connected with Scully, not just for who she was but also for what she'd overcome. This is a woman who has been abducted and experimented on by aliens, discovers that she is infertile, watches the child she didn't know she could have die, gets kidnapped multiple times, faces death on more than one occasion, and deals with the flukeman (a genetic mutant that found its way into the New Jersey sewer system and is something she tells Mulder she could have done without). Yet she survives all of this and even thrives. Is it any wonder that fans, like this one, saw Scully as a source of hope:

> I was a teenager when it wrapped up in 2002. I was a suicidal emo teenager who had no friends. *The X-Files* was not only a

---

12   Jones 2012.

TV show to me, but a comfort and a lifeline. The way that I'd make it through the day would be "well, if Scully can get through the academy with all this testosterone and have the kind of amazing attitude that she has, then I can too".

In a panel at the 2013 New York Comic Con that celebrated the show's twentieth anniversary, Anderson talked about the surprise success of the show and how her character had inspired women to go into STEM, saying

> I had no idea. It was a surprise to me when I was told that. We got a lot of letters all the time, and I was told quite frequently by girls who were going into the medical world or the science world or the FBI world or other worlds that I reigned, that they were pursuing those pursuits because of the character of Scully. And I said, "Yay!"[13]

The "Scully effect" was cited by many female fans who responded to my questionnaire about the show's revival. Some, teenagers or in their early twenties when the show aired, had adopted the ideals of Scully and the feminist leanings of the show, like this fan, who wrote, "Scully is my role model in life. The Scully effect affected my life in a very good way: I'm an independent, strong woman who is also a feminist and who wants to achieve her dreams and never gives up." Others talked about the effect the show had on their career choices, like this fan, who said, "*The X-Files* was a huge part of my preteen years. I am a direct result of the Scully effect. I majored in criminal justice and work in law enforcement." In fact, the number of fans who said they were influenced by Scully and the series surprised even me—someone whose entire career has been shaped by the show (albeit in a different way). Fans dyed their hair red, adopted Scully's mannerisms, got their doctorates, decided to work in law enforcement, studied medicine, joined the military, and became doctors because of Scully—and those

---

13   Selby. 2018. "'The Scully Effect' Is Real—and There's Data to Prove It." *Global Citizen*.

were just the 2,000-some fans who responded to my surveys.

The Scully effect is not just anecdotal, though. In 2018, the Geena Davis Institute on Gender in Media undertook a systematic study of the influence of Scully on girls and women in STEM. The institute was seeking to determine whether Scully's character improved women's perceptions of STEM fields, whether she inspired girls and women to go into a STEM profession, and whether female viewers saw Scully as a role model. Women are underrepresented in STEM both in the US and globally. When the research was carried out, women made up 48 percent of the college-educated workforce in the US but held only 24 percent of the jobs in STEM. Only 10 percent of the graduate degrees earned by women were in STEM fields, compared with 24 percent of the graduate degrees earned by men. These figures come from 2018, so we can see how rare a character like Scully was in 1993. There are a variety of reasons for this gender gap, ranging from a lack of encouragement by parents and teachers to gender discrimination within the fields themselves. But one interesting reason cited was "a stereotype frequently rendered in entertainment media: that of a lone, 'nerdy' scientist in a lab coat, commonly portrayed as a 'mad scientist' or a socially awkward white man."[14] Enter Dana Scully. The survey conducted by the Geena Davis Institute was answered by over 2,000 women, most of whom were aged forty or older (so were likely to have seen *The X-Files* as teenagers or young adults, rather than in syndication or on streaming channels later). Of the 2,000-plus sample, though, 49 percent had studied a STEM subject in college or were working in STEM.

Although I could, I'm not going to go into the details here of what the report found. It's available online and makes for interesting reading. What the study did find, though, was strong scientific evidence for the Scully effect. Women who regularly watched the show were 50 percent more likely to have worked in STEM than those who didn't, with 63 percent of those women saying Scully had served as their role model. As Anderson herself said, *The X-Files*, through Scully, "manifested a

---

14   Geena Davis Institute on Gender in Media. 2018. *The Scully Effect: I Want to Believe in STEM.*

woman not yet depicted on TV, and as the fan response soon proved, a desperately needed role model for women of all ages, everywhere."[15] *The X-Files* was a pioneering show in terms of gender representation, and while it didn't do well in all areas, as I've mentioned, its impact can't be denied. Even with the issues that had beset the show by the end of season nine, discussed elsewhere in this book, the show is considered an influential series because of Scully, and new viewers also connect with the character, suggesting that the struggles Scully faced and her attitude in overcoming them are relevant across all ages and generations.

15   Ibid.

CHAPTER 9

Gender and Sexuality in the Twenty-First Century

"You can't transform into a different sex; that's nuts!"
- Guy Mann ("Mulder and Scully Meet the Weremonster")

The X-Files had proved that a strong female character could be successful and paved the way for other well-written women on TV. It also had a real-world impact, showing that it was possible for a woman to be a successful FBI agent, doctor, or scientist or to succeed in any other career. Yet by the time the revival seasons came around—some sixteen years after the end of the series and eight years after the second film—society had dramatically changed. I mentioned in the last chapter how disappointing it was that the first time we see a gay character on the show was in season seven, which ran between 1999 and 2000, but broadly speaking, by 2000 and into the 2010s, gay, lesbian, and queer characters were becoming far more common on the small screen. *Will & Grace*, which originally ran from 1998 to 2006, featured two gay men in central roles, just living their lives while also happening to be gay, as well as a bisexual woman. *Buffy the Vampire Slayer* (1997-2001) saw Willow enter a relatively happy lesbian relationship with Tara, although the less said about the ending, the better. Series like The *L-Word* and *Glee* also normalized queer relationships on television, while Netflix's *Sense8* was not only written by transgender writers (the Wachowski sisters, most famous for *The Matrix*) but also featured a diverse cast of queer characters.

This reflected the changing attitudes to gender and sexuality in the US, the UK, and across the globe that took place in the 2000s. Serving as openly gay in the military became legal in the UK in 2000, while by 2004 same-sex marriage was recognized at a federal level in the US, although not legally recognized by all states. In the UK, same-sex marriage became legal in 2014 (previously same sex-couples could have a civil partnership), while same-sex adoptions were recognized at the federal level in the US in 2015, and the right to change legal gender without surgery being required became legal under federal law in 2017, though some states still required surgery. Given these changes, both on-screen and off, we might have expected *The X-Files* to adopt a similarly progressive approach, but representation hadn't improved in either *I Want to Believe* or seasons ten and eleven. In fact, for some fans and critics, it had gotten worse.

XXX

While *I Want to Believe* doesn't really come under the heading of revival, it was an important chapter in the life of *The X-Files*. Carter had been planning for the film since 2001, but a variety of factors meant that development didn't start until 2007. By this point, fans' disappointment with the final seasons had eased somewhat, and the fact that the film would be more like a monster-of-the-week episode than one driven by the mythology of the series was also well received. In the film, Mulder and Scully reunite to help the FBI investigate the disappearances of several women. So far, so normal; disappearing women are not unusual on the show. Yet Mulder and Scully are joined by Father Joe, a priest who was kicked out of the church for molesting altar boys and who claims that he is experiencing psychic visions that can help the investigation. We discover the women were being abducted by an organ transporter called Janke Dacyshyn so that their body parts could be used to keep his husband, Franz Tomczeszyn, alive. It turns out that both Dacyshyn and Tomczeszyn were among the boys sexually abused by Father Joe. Unsurprisingly, while fans loved seeing Mulder and Scully back together, the rest of the plot was heavily criticized for being homophobic and transphobic. While I'm sure this wasn't intentional, it definitely seems shortsighted. Detective Drummy tells Mulder and Scully the link between their suspects and Father Joe, saying, "That's one of his thirty-seven altar boys. Three guesses who he's married to in the state of Massachusetts. Our suspect." Same-sex marriage was made legal in Massachusetts in 2004, but the way in which Drummy says it—or the context in which it's mentioned—isn't presented as a particularly positive framing of the changing attitudes to equal rights.

What's more disturbing, though, is the use of female victims to create a new body for Tomczeszyn. Tomczeszyn is a man who doesn't identify in any other way over the course of the film. Why would he want his head transplanted onto a new body? This again seems to fall back on deeply troubling tropes that suggest gay men really want to be women or, as Alexander Stevenson writes, "that he's 'not really gay'—that he's only been acting that way because of the childhood sexual abuse at the hands of another of the movie's characters."[1] I asked fans what they thought of *I Want to Believe* when season ten was announced, and the responses overwhelmingly highlighted how Carter and Spotnitz had dropped the ball in terms of representation. One fan pointed out that "the inclusion of a gay murderer harvesting body parts for his lover to transition to a woman aided bad stereotypes and reeked of trans/homophobia," while another said they hated it so much they almost walked out of the theater. Responding to fans' criticism on his blog, Spotnitz did apologize for any offense the film had caused:

> While it's true the villains in this story happen to be gay, it
> was not our intention to suggest that being gay, transgender

---

1   Stevenson. 2008. "The Homophobia is out there in new *X-Files* movie." *Logo TV.*

or a victim of pedophilia is in any way villainous. It should go without saying that nothing could be farther from the truth. The sexual orientation of the villains, their connection to Father Joe, and the motive for their crimes were all intended to deepen the mystery, not to make any kind of moral judgment. In truth, theirs is a love story that is meant to parallel Scully's story (the lengths that both will go to save a loved one, the not-so-coincidental overlap in scientific research, etc.). If we have offended anyone, you have my deepest apology.[2]

I Want to Believe clearly draws on earlier influences, as do many of *The X-Files*'s episodes, including *Frankenstein* (see "Post-Modern Prometheus") and *Silence of the Lambs* (itself criticized for being transphobic). In a Movie Blog review of the film, though, Darren points out, "Given how much cultural sensitivity and awareness had progressed in the years since *The Silence of the Lambs*, it is quite surprising that Carter and Spotnitz could be so oblivious to the subtext of their gigantic homage."[3] And that's a fair point. Despite the fact that the film was dedicated to Randy Stone, *The X-Files*'s original casting director and cofounder of the Trevor Project, a support group for LGBT youth, the text of the film was firmly in the nineties, including its stereotypical representation of gay men. The hope then, when season ten was announced, was that the series would become more progressive and include more diverse representations of gender, race, and sexuality.

The revival seasons didn't quite live up to that expectation, though. We meet a gay man in "Founder's Mutation," although hearing his sexuality referred to by Scully as "his lifestyle preferences" misses the point completely. Similarly, while we did see some characters of color, their representation wasn't, unfortunately, progressive. For example, the season's second episode, "Babylon," features Muslim suicide bombers. While I can see what Carter was trying to do—making a caricature

---

2   Spotnitz. 2008. "Homophobia?" *Big Light.*

3   The M0vie Blog. 2016. "Non-Review Review: *The X-Files–I Want to Believe.*"

of those who since 9/11 have accused the Muslim community of wanting to "wipe you and America off the map. To honor their hero, Osama bin Laden, whose picture we find all too frequently on their refrigerators," to quote the episode's Special Agent Brem—"Babylon" falls a bit flat. Instead of pointing out how absurd those beliefs are or reflecting on the political climate under Trump (as I talked about in Chapter Three), it instead maintains stereotypes of Muslims as attackers and Islam as a religion of violence. Stereotypes are again at play in the third episode, written by Darin Morgan (whose work I've gushed about already in this book). In "Mulder and Scully Meet the Were-Monster," the pair are in search of a lizardman who appears to be roaming around a small town and brutally killing people. There are lots of things to love about this episode, not least the reference to former *X-Files* director and producer Kim Manners, who passed away in 2009. Fans who responded to my survey overwhelmingly said this episode was the best of the season and that the inclusion of Easter eggs and references to the early seasons made it stand out. I loved all of those things, but they were unfortunately overshadowed by the way that Annabel, a transgender prostitute, is depicted. The character is clearly intended to be transgender—in a somewhat odd conversation when Mulder and Scully are interviewing her about being attacked by the monster, she tells them it was wearing "tighty-whities. Same kind I used to wear. I transitioned last year." On the one hand, it's great that we see a transgender character in the show. On the other, it's bizarre that she would openly tell law enforcement that she transitioned, especially given the number of transgender people of color who are killed each year. One of the first people killed by police following the death of George Floyd, sparking the 2020 Black Lives Matter protests, was Tony McDade, a thirty-eight-year-old Black transgender man. In fact, as Rodrigo Heng-Lehtinen of the National Center for Transgender Equality told *The Independent*, "Transgender people of colour are much more likely to face this kind of harassment and outright violence from white police officers than other people. They're much more likely to be stopped. They're much more likely, especially Black trans women, are so much likely to be suspected of doing sex work."[4] And there we have the second issue with the character of Annabel: she *is* doing sex work.

This might be played for laughs in the episode, but it comes across as very transphobic, drawing on the fetishization of trans people as taboo sex objects and ignoring the fact that transgender women of color are sometimes forced into sex work as a result of poverty. A fan who commented on the episode pointed out the various issues they found with it:

> The best episode of the bunch (but that's a very low bar to reach). I love writer Darin Morgan's episodes in the original series run, so I had very high hopes for this one. Overall, it was very good; it was funny and engaging and I loved the callbacks to the original series (Mulder's red speedo, the two stoners, "Mulder, it's me," Scully's immortality, etc.). However, the episode has two major flaws. First, its transmisogyny: the episode featured a sex worker who was a trans woman (strike one: presenting a stereotypical portrayal of a trans sex worker; strike two: allowing a cisgender man to play the role of a trans woman) and many of the episode's jokes relied on her "past as a man" (strike three).

Not only do some of the later jokes rely on her past as a man, but transitioning seems to be equated to werewolf myths and other stories of humans transforming into animals. Mulder tries to explain this to the were-monster, and to be fair, he explains the process in a fairly matter-of-fact manner:

> MULDER: She used to be . . . she once . . . she's transgender.
> GUY: What? You can't transform into a different sex! That's nuts!
> MULDER: It's not nuts, actually a very common medical procedure. You don't need the surgery, technically, to—
> GUY: Maybe that's what I could do! It's a cure! I'll do

4   Marcus. 2021. "The deadly epidemic we must acknowledge this Pride–the murder of transgender people of colour." *The Independent*.

the surgery!
MULDER: No, completely different.
GUY: Tell me how much it costs, I'll do it.
MULDER: They cut off your genitals.
GUY: No, leave it. That's a step too far, isn't it?

But the fact that the punchline to this conversation is that "they cut off your genitals" misses the point completely. Transitioning is not simply about genitals (some trans people don't have gender reassignment surgery at all), and to reduce the topic to that while also equating it to monster transformation myths seems like a very odd, and not particularly progressive, choice.

XXX

Perhaps the biggest areas in which fans were hoping for some improvement was with Scully, though. Fans who responded to my questionnaire were still salty about the William storyline in seasons eight and nine and were divided on whether they actually wanted this to be returned to. One fan said they wanted Carter to deal with the storyline in a way that did justice to the characters given what Scully had gone through. Others hoped that we'd seen the last of "the devil child." Scully's earlier pregnancy and William were key features of season ten, though, with the second episode, "Founder's Mutation," showing Mulder and Scully discussing their fears that William was infected with alien DNA. Later episodes like "Home Again" and "My Struggle II" also focused heavily on Scully's guilt in giving him up for adoption and on the eventual realization that it is only stem cells from William, who does have alien DNA, that will save Mulder from the mass extinction threatening humanity. For the fans who had wanted season ten to return to the mytharc, the way it was done was underwhelming. One fan felt the season's emphasis on Scully as mother took away from the fact that William was also Mulder's son, while another told me, "I thought the episodes suffered a bit from Chris Carter's heavy-handedness and the usual 'women are just incubators' kind of schtick that always irritated me." Fans had hoped for a return to the Scully we knew from previous seasons, when she was strong, confident, and self-assured. But they also wanted to see a pushback against the misogyny that had been increasingly evident in the real world over the last few years. The decade had seen a campaign of harassment of women in the video game industry, with death and rape threats sent to women who simply pointed out that misogyny exists and men could do better. Donald Trump had been elected president after a campaign in which his misogynistic comments about grabbing women "by the pussy" were released, and scores of marches protesting against him took place across the US. While season ten might not have quite given fans the Scully they wanted, there was still hope that the longer season eleven would.

The season opened with the revelation that it was Cigarette Smoking Man, rather than Mulder, who is William's father. In flashback to the seventh-season episode "En Ami," we see Cigarette Smoking Man arrive at a house with a sleeping Scully in the car. In the original episode, Scully accuses Cigarette Smoking Man of drugging her; in this episode, we find out that he did. Discussing the events with Skinner in "My Struggle III," Cigarette Smoking Man admits that he "impregnated Scully with alien science" and that he is William's father. I have to admit that watching this at the time, I was shocked. The William storyline had never really been that well thought out, but to have Cigarette Smoking Man medically rape Scully and to feature it in a show being aired in 2018 seemed absolutely insane. And I wasn't the only one. Fans who talked to me about the reaction to the season overwhelmingly talked about this storyline and how upset they were with Carter. One wrote:

> I thought they were desecrating everything that came before. Chris Carter ret-conned a significant storyline in ways that I found unbelievable, disturbing and needlessly cruel. My Struggle III included the repeated physical brutalization of the Scully character, which is a well that Chris Carter dips into way too often for my liking. Also to tell a story in which Scully has been raped; to not call it that; and to not provide a scene in which she is told this information and given the opportunity to speak about it, was reprehensible. It would be

reprehensible anyway, but especially in this day and age of "Me Too," it is completely tone deaf.

Another felt that it turned Scully from a well-rounded character into a trope so that her womanhood was just another plot point to advance the show.

These reactions shouldn't come as a surprise. In the last two chapters, I've detailed not only how *The X-Files* was progressive in terms of gender representation, but also the extent to which fans—especially female fans—connected to Scully. She is a role model, someone fans look up to and in some cases model themselves on, and the treatment of the William storyline seemed to wipe all of that out. These reactions were only heightened after Carter defended the decision. In an interview with *Entertainment Weekly*, he stated that he'd known since season seven that Cigarette Smoking Man had drugged and impregnated Scully (contradicting an earlier interview with Frank Spotnitz, who had confirmed the writers all thought Mulder was the father), but when asked if that meant Cigarette Smoking Man was William's literal father, he said, "He's the figurative father if he's not the actual father. He didn't rape Scully. He impregnated her with science."[5] The trouble is that is rape. Scully was drugged, unconscious, and unable to consent. Just because Cigarette Smoking Man didn't have sex with Scully doesn't mean she wasn't raped, and Carter's refusal to accept or understand that made fans angry. As one fan wrote:

> Overall, I just felt like Carter was stubbornly sticking to a plot that was valued more for shock value than for meaningful storytelling, and at the expense of his characters and alienating the audience, many of whom stopped watching in disgust after the ending of My Struggle III and never came back. He seems unwilling to adapt to the times and unwilling to admit to potential errors in judgment. He just seems very out of touch with his characters, his actors, and his audience these

5   Hibberd. 2018. "*The X-Files* creator defends shocking premiere twist." *Entertainment Weekly*.

days, and that's really unfortunate.

What seemed even more frustrating was that Scully being impregnated against her knowledge had been acknowledged as medical rape on the show itself in season five. It also seemed pointless as far as the alien DNA storyline goes—we've known since William was born that he had the ability to operate alien technology and move objects with his mind. Even more troubling, though, was the idea that Carter would proceed with this storyline in the midst of the #MeToo movement and discussions about the sexual harassment of women in the entertainment industry.

In 2017, after Harvey Weinstein was the subject of numerous sexual abuse allegations, the hashtag #MeToo began circulating on social media. A number of high-profile celebrities tweeted or posted about their experiences of sexual harassment in Hollywood. Jennifer Lawrence spoke about her experiences at *Elle* magazine's Women in Hollywood event, and Uma Thurman called out Harvey Weinstein on her Instagram account. Sexual abuse allegations in Hollywood aren't new, but the #MeToo movement brought renewed attention to older cases of sexual abuse as well as encouraging conversation about sexual harassment. Given this focus on women's experiences and the ways that power, sex, and abuse can be linked, fans were astounded that Carter wouldn't have taken this into account, especially when he seemed so aware of other current issues:

And yet again we have medical rape. It's getting old. That might have been acceptable in the 90's, but it's 2018 and women are sick of those stories. CC, who seems to understand the times we're living in (Trump, deep state, Dr. They!) missed the #MeToo movement completely.

On the other hand, fans had been critical of Carter's writing for some time (many were concerned about his involvement with the revival seasons and felt it would have been better for him to stay at arm's length and let someone like Frank Spotnitz take the reins). For these fans, the medical rape storyline was disappointing but not shocking given what else Scully had gone through over the past ten seasons:

> In a way, I wasn't shocked that CC chose to go down that route. But given the current climate of #MeToo and various movements for more equal representations, and choosing a medical rape storyline and then going to insist that it's not was a line crossed too far for me to even defend.

That so many fans highlighted the #MeToo movement showed how out of touch Carter was in failing to take account of discussions that were happening around sexual harassment, gender equality, and the depiction of women in the media. Felix Brinker argues that a revival is "not simply a continuation of a television narrative that has ceased to unfold, but an attempt to reboot the larger cultural mobilizations that clustered around it in the past."[6] *The X-Files* had been lauded for its depiction of Scully as a strong female character, but this depiction seemed to falter in the revival, which was made doubly frustrating given that Anderson spoke out about the fact she'd had to fight to receive the same pay as Duchovny. Again.

XXX

The revival seasons of *The X-Files* showed us that while some things had changed, others had very much stayed the same. Although some women writers were hired on the original series, they never seemed to last more than a year.[7] The first time a woman had directed an episode of the show was in season seven when Anderson wrote and directed "all things" (the second was season nine's "John Doe," directed by Michelle Maclaren, who would go on to work on *The Walking Dead*). An effort to involve a more diverse crew behind the scenes took place in season eleven only after critics, including Anderson herself, highlighted the

---

6   Brinker. 2018. "Conspiracy, Procedure, Continuity: Reopening *The X-Files*." *Television & New Media*, 19(4), p. 328.

7   Kim Newton, who was a writer during season three, talked about her experience on the "historically male" show with *Buzzfeed News*'s Susan Cheng.

fact that none of the writers or directors for season ten were women.[8] Sharing a link on Twitter to a *Washington Post* article that criticized the all-male writing team, Anderson wrote, "And 2 out of 207 eps directed by women. I too look forward to the day when the numbers are different. #TheFutureisFemale." Dana Walden, Fox's CEO, told a Television Critics Association panel that Carter had assigned two episodes to women writers and was "making moves in the right direction," adding that the writers were hired "before news broke of this particular situation."[9] Three female writers ended up writing two episodes, with two female directors also added to the crew.

Despite this addition, however, neither season ten or eleven were as progressive or as groundbreaking as fans had hoped they would be. The season eleven finale ended with Scully, a fifty-four-year-old infertile woman, announcing she was pregnant shortly after Cigarette Smoking Man shot and—from Mulder and Scully's point of view—killed William:

> SCULLY: He wanted us to let him go. He wasn't meant to be.
> MULDER: William was our son.
> SCULLY: No.
> MULDER: Scully, he was our son.
> SCULLY: No. William was an experiment, Mulder.
> MULDER: What are you talking about?
> SCULLY: Mulder. He was an idea, born in a laboratory.
> MULDER: But you were his mother.
> SCULLY: No. I carried him. And I bore him. But I was never a mother to him. I wasn't. William . . . William was—
> MULDER: But for so long I believed. What am I now if I'm not a father?
> SCULLY: You are a father.
> MULDER: What are you talking about? That's impossible.
> SCULLY: I know. I know it is. It's more than impossible.

8   Carter did, however, share a story credit with Dr. Anne Simon and Dr. Margaret Fearon, who consulted on the season-ten finale, "My Struggle II."

9   Desta. 2017. "So the *X-Files* Revival Hired Female Writers and Directors After All." *Vanity Fair*.

Fans were, on the whole, incensed with this development, arguing that it reduced Scully to nothing more than a vessel for "baby-making," that it minimized the grief she went through in giving up William for adoption, and that it was out of character for her to dismiss William so easily. In responding to criticisms of the episode, Carter argued that it wasn't outside the realm of "extreme possibility" for a woman in her fifties to get pregnant,[10] but even Anderson seemed to agree with the critics. On March 23, 2018, two days after the season finale aired, she tweeted a GIF of Scully covering her face in disbelief along with the text "Oh boy oh boy do I ever hear you," and when asked at the 2018 Wizard World convention what *The X-Files* would have been like if it had been written from a more feminist perspective, she said, "There would probably be less focus on her reproductive . . . it would be less of an obsession."[11] Shifting attitudes to gender and sexuality in the twenty-first century hadn't necessarily been reflected in the revival seasons, a shame in a series which had previously been so good at recognizing the issues of its time.

10   Gennis. 2018. "*The X-Files* Finale: Creator Talks Scully's Shocking Ending and Where the Series Goes Next." *TV Guide.*

11   Dulanto. 2019. "Dana Scully's Truth is Still Out There: On *The X-Files* Finale, Gaslighting, and Unexplored Narratives." *Dismantle Magazine.*

SECTION FOUR

DENY EVERYTHING

CHAPTER 10

Cult TV, Quality TV, and the New Golden Age of Television

"I don't think it's live television, Scully. She just said *bleep*."
– Mulder ("X-Cops")

T he television landscape in the late eighties and early nineties was markedly different from what we have now. While genre-specific channels like Comedy Central, MTV, and the Cartoon Network had launched in the 1980s, and subscription services like HBO and Showtime were expanding, the overall US market was dominated by three networks: ABC, CBS, and NBC. *Great,* you might be thinking to yourself, *but what's this got to do with The X-Files?* While this isn't a book on the history of US television and its industrial contexts, the changes to how TV was made between the 1950s and the mid-2000s are relevant to why the series was picked up by Fox, its resulting success, and the influence it had on later television shows. The first era of television we need to be concerned with is referred to in academic work as TVI, or the "network era," and is broadly thought of as the period between the early 1950s and the mid-1980s. This era was dominated by the networks mentioned above, relatively few programs were available for viewing, and those that did air were designed to appeal to a mass audience. In the very early years of this period, much of the programming aired live and was produced in New York; the Hollywood studios saw television as a threat to their business and wanted nothing to do with it. Some historians refer to this rather romantically as television's first "Golden Age," and in fact many extraordinary character-driven anthology dramas did air during this period, from the typewriters of such acclaimed dramatists as Paddy Chayefsky, Reginald Rose, and Rod Serling (who successfully made the transition to filmed television in the late fifties and early sixties with *The Twilight Zone*), but there was no shortage either of forgettable, cheaply produced programming churned out to meet the needs of a burgeoning medium with a rapacious appetite (including quiz shows, which were tarnished when producers and sponsors were found to be fixing the outcomes). Nevertheless, these programs, along with such comedy gems as *Your Show of Shows* and *The Honeymooners*, played a crucial role in establishing television as a "vital technology of cultural citizenship amid the changing landscape of postwar America."[1] In the beginning, most of the TV sets in America were found in homes in major cities, which led the networks to greenlight certain ethnic programming (*The Goldbergs, Amos 'n Andy*) targeted at urban audiences. However, when the FCC freeze on the awarding of new station licenses was lifted in 1951 and Hollywood studios—led by Disney and Warner Bros.—finally started to recognize the economic opportunities television presented, TV ownership quickly spread across the country. Still, most homes had only one TV set, so viewing was a shared experience, and the networks naturally targeted broad audiences, presenting programming that was more homogeneous, safer, and less provocative. As Amanda D. Lotz points out, across all three networks, "Challenging, unconventional, or contentious 'edgy' content were planed from programming to avoid alienating

---

1   Kackman. 2018. "Television Before the Classic Network Era: 1930s-1950s." In Aniko Bodroghkozy (ed) *A Companion to American Broadcasting*. John Wiley & Sons, pp.76-77.

family audiences."² Sponsors, who were ponying up the dollars to pay for television programming through thirty- or sixty-second ads, preferred it that way too: the more eyeballs a show drew, the more people saw their commercials, all of which added up to this: comfort food, good; controversy, bad. Hence, television during this time also played a central role in "naturalizing the nuclear family ideal, selling suburbanisation [and] sustaining cold war paranoia"³—all concepts that are visited, and subverted, throughout *The X-Files*.

As technology developed during the early 1980s, viewers found themselves with many more choices and much more control over what they watched—and when they watched it. With the introduction of VCRs and remote controls, audiences could watch when they wanted to rather than when the network told them to, and the explosion of cable channels meant that the three-network hegemony was under siege. This new, multichannel era, also known as TVII, coincided with a de-emphasis on overall ratings and a new focus on demographic ratings, meaning young, urban professionals who had enough money to spend on advertised products and were perceived as less likely to be restrained from trying new products by brand loyalty. This, then, encouraged at least some of the networks to embrace programming ideas by a new breed of creator/showrunner, peddlers of more challenging, provocative shows. Typically, it was the last-place network that was willing to take the most risks. Hence, as Bambi Haggins and Julia Himberg write, "Series such as *Murder She Wrote* (1984–96) sought to keep [CBS's] graying audience happy with non-threatening 'whodunits'" and NBC was 'riding high' due to "its 'Must See TV' line up in the late 1980s with *The Cosby Show* (1984–92), *Cheers* (1982–93) and *LA Law* (1986–94)."⁴ When ABC dropped into the cellar, it greenlighted shows like yuppie-angst drama

---

2   Lotz. 2009. "What Is U.S. Television Now?" *The Annals of the American Academy of Political and Social Science* 625.1, p. 52. Lotz has written extensively about television for those interested in the history, industrial operation, and cultural contexts of the medium in the US.

3   Reeves, Rodgers, and Epstein. 1996. "Rewriting Popularity: The Cult Files." In David Lavery, Angela Hague and Marla Cartwright (eds) *Deny All Knowledge: Reading The X-Files*. Faber and Faber, p. 25.

4   Haggins and Himberg. 2018. "The Multi-Channel Transition Period, 1980s–1990s." In Aniko Bodroghkozy (ed) *A Companion to American Broadcasting*. John Wiley & Sons, p. 113.

thirtysomething (1987–91) and Mark Frost and David Lynch's surreal brew of nighttime soap, mystery, and horror, *Twin Peaks* (1990–91).[5] In the midst of all this change, a new network appeared, offering an alternative to the three existing networks, with a different kind of programming. The Fox Broadcasting Company, a subsidiary of 20th Century Fox, went on the air in October 1986, featuring a combination of original shows like *Married . . . with Children*, *21 Jump Street*, and *The Simpsons*, which were seen as edgier than much of the programming being offered by the other three networks, targeting an even younger audience and setting a "trajectory for its brand as young, bold and irreverent."[6] After conducting focus groups throughout the US in spring 1986, Fox executives concluded that they needed to develop programming that could explore the limits of genre and push the boundaries of storytelling in order to make a dent in the ratings and thus attract sponsors. This is where producers like Carter came in.

XXX

A graduate of California State University, Carter began writing for Surfing magazine and worked there for thirteen years before moving over to television. He began by writing for Walt Disney Studios, on such *Disney Sunday Movie* installments as *The B.R.A.T. Patrol* and *Meet the Munceys*, but his real interest was in writing serious drama. After meeting NBC programming whiz Brandon Tartikoff at a softball game, Carter was invited to write for the network; while he did wind up scripting several pilots, none was produced (he did, however, land a job as producer on the short-lived musical comedy/drama *Rags to Riches*). One of Carter's unproduced scripts was read by Peter Roth, who shortly after became head of Fox's television production wing and hired Carter to develop a new series for the network. Carter was intent on creating something different both from his own previous work and from what was airing on TV at the time. Having watched

---

5   Ibid.

6   Ibid.

The Twilight Zone, The Outer Limits and *Kolchak: The Night Stalker*
as a child and being "scared out of his wits," he decided to focus on
creating a series that was both frightening and sophisticated. Hence,
The X-Files.

Carter's interest in creating a mytharc involving aliens was
sparked by the work of Harvard psychiatrist Dr. John Mack, who
had undertaken a study of men and women who reported alien
encounters and published the results in a book called *Abduction:
Human Encounters with Aliens*. Mack found that there were aspects of
these experiences that could be justifiably taken literally, which Carter
found fascinating:

> This man in the highest levels of academia and a scientist using
> rigorous scientific methods had come up with something
> quite astounding. So I thought that was a wonderful entry
> into explorations of the paranormal. And so I came up with
> Mulder and Scully, the FBI, and this fictional investigative
> unit called the X-Files.[7]

Grounding the show in reality and making it credible was important
from the start. Partnering Mulder, the believer, with Scully, the skeptic,
offered viewers a counterpoint to the paranormal goings-on, and
positioning them in the FBI, which had previously investigated real-
life allegations of satanic and ritual murders, made the investigation
process believable. Already, then, *The X-Files* was becoming difficult to
classify, and difficult to sell. Carter wrote an outline for a pilot episode
and pitched it to Bob Greenblatt, then head of programming for Fox,
who turned the proposal down:

> We had a blind deal with Chris. We thought he was going to
> pitch a family or teenage soap, so we were surprised when he
> brought us high-concept science fiction. We were reluctant to
> develop it because we didn't have any other drama like it and

---

7   Vitaris. 1995. "X-Files: Pushing Horror's Envelope," *Cinefantastique*, p. 22.

weren't in the market for sci-fi.[8]

Fox was smaller than the Big Three networks, with fewer national affiliates, and had fewer hours of programming to fill. Most of its affiliated stations at first were located in urban areas. All of these factors led to a mandate to create shows that spoke to a younger and more diverse demographic than ABC, CBS, and NBC were targeting. Sandy Grushow, president of the network at the time, was on the lookout for "whatever the Fox version of a procedural could be."[9] Carter's second pitch to Greenblatt, which convinced him that the paranormal elements of *The X-Files* would be handled in a realistic way, was successful.

Looking at the context in which the show was created, academics Rogers, Epstein, and Reeves point out that Fox initially conceived of *The X-Files* "as a candidate for cult status, hoping that the relatively small avid viewership of the program would gradually build to a respectable large audience,"[10] although the network would have been "perfectly happy" if the program became a top ten show. *The X-Files* was one of two hourlong series that premiered on Fox in September 1993, along with a western, *The Adventures of Brisco County Jr.*, which Fox thought would be the more popular show. *The X-Files* was thus scheduled for Friday nights at nine, immediately after *Brisco County*, in the hope that viewers would stay along for the ride. In hindsight, this strategy was successful—for *The X-Files*, at least: while *Brisco County* was canceled after one season, viewing figures for *The X-Files* kept rising as the season progressed. And it wasn't simply the relationship between the two leads or the ingenious blurring of genres that attracted viewers. The show looked great, with remarkable production values for television, which many others shows have sought to duplicate since. Douglas Kellner, talking about the production, writes:

---

8   O'Connell. 2016. "When *The X-Files* Became A-List: An Oral History of Fox's Out-There Success Story." *Hollywood Reporter.*

9   Ibid.

10   Reeves, et. al. 1996, p. 31.

The use of lighting and framing is often highly expressionistic, producing aesthetic images and effects rarely experienced in network television. The moving camera and fluid editing provide visual pleasure in the flow of images, and the show revels in novel sights, sounds, and narrative sequences. In general, the series is exceptionally well made, and the result is aesthetically innovative and thematically challenging texts that are rather unique in the history of mainstream television.[11]

The show also benefited from extremely gifted writers who concocted compelling, ingenious storylines. In the first season, writing partners Glen Morgan and James Wong joined the team, along with Howard Gordon and Alex Gansa; Morgan and Wong had worked on *21 Jump Street* and *The Commish*, while Gordon and Gansa had worked on *Beauty and the Beast*. The ranges of their talents enabled *The X-Files*'s too expand beyond the alien-abduction and government-conspiracy storylines that we see in the first two episodes Episode three, written by Morgan and Wong, explored a genetic mutant who came out of hibernation every sixty years to kill. "Squeeze" has become one of the show's most recognizable episodes; both the *Vancouver Sun* and *The A.V. Club* called it one of the best stand-alone episodes of the series. While retaining elements of the police procedural, "Squeeze" is the first episode that could be categorized as horror rather than science fiction. Two episodes later, "Jersey Devil" addressed the folklore of New Jersey. This mixture of serial narrative—the overarching mytharc—and stand-alone, monster-of-the-week episodes, theoretically appealed to both casual viewers and those more invested in the storyline, but in practice a niche audience of engaged viewers—or fans—was targeted. Catherine Johnson argues that this, along with the series's generic hybridity, willingness to examine contemporary issues, and signature moody lighting created a new type of television that she calls "quality/cult," which "combined quality television's dual address

---

11   Kellner 1999, p. 164.

to the 'everyday' and 'discerning' viewer, with an additional address to the fan-consumer."[12] Fox had its cult hit, and critics were equally enthusiastic. The audience kept growing, as did its passion for the show, thanks in part to the early online fan communities, as I talk about in Chapter Twelve.

XXX

Of course, *The X-Files* wasn't the first show to blur the lines between different genres, develop a uniquely artful visual style, and emerge as a cult hit with a passionate fan base. In Mark Frost and David Lynch's *Twin Peaks*, which premiered on ABC in April 1990, FBI Special Agent Dale Cooper investigates the murder of a local teenager, Laura Palmer, in the town of Twin Peaks, Washington. While on paper the series sounds like a conventional police procedural, in actuality it merged multiple genres, including soap opera, horror, supernatural, and murder mystery into a surreal serial narrative. Initial response was hugely positive, but there was no denying it "challenged the expectations and tolerance of 1990s television viewers,"[13] and once Palmer's murder was resolved in the second season, the show rapidly lost viewers and was soon canceled. While *Twin Peaks* may not have been considered a commercial success at the time, its influence can't be denied, especially its visual style—more akin to what was seen in film than on television. This visual style was perhaps most evident in the season two finale, where the audience spends twenty minutes watching Cooper's almost silent journey through the increasingly strange Red Room. David Chase (*The Sopranos*), Damon Lindelof (*Lost, The Leftovers, Watchmen*), and Donald Glover (*Atlanta*) are just a few of the many accomplished showrunners who have cited *Twin Peaks* as an influence on their work. While the show's surreality and the onus it placed on the audience to decode the symbolism in

---

12   Johnson 2005, p. 63.

13   McCarthy. 2017. "How *Twin Peaks* Brought Viewers Existential Mobsters and Advertising Doppelgängers." In Eric Hoffman and Dominick Grace (eds) *Approaching Twin Peaks Critical Essays on the Original Series*. McFarland, p. 3.

order to follow what was happening appealed to some viewers, its quick cancellation perhaps offered a lesson in what would and would not work when appealing to a larger audience—yes, demographics were more important than overall ratings, but this was still broadcast TV. *Twin Peaks*'s influence on *The X-Files* is evident. Superficially, each features FBI agents investigating strange phenomena in small-town America. Both were filmed in the Pacific Northwest and so have a similar visual feel, and both utilized some of the same actors (Duchovny appeared in *Twin Peaks* season two as DEA Agent Denise Bryson). Yet, as Zack Handlen and Emily Todd Vanderwerff point out, "The element *The X-Files* adopted most from *Twin Peaks* [was] a willingness to take its time with the *look* of a series, to come up with visual ways to tell its stories."[14] Lynch may have used his background in film to develop the visual style of *Twin Peaks*, but Carter applied that look to a show that combined serial and stand-alone stories, circumventing some of the issues that had led to ratings issues for *Twin Peaks* and in the process—according to the 1997 Peabody Award judges—producing an "innovative and creative dramatic series which is reinvigorating the form and bringing new vitality to prime-time television entertainment."[15] *The X-Files* became one of the most influential shows of the early 1990s, inspiring countless others in one way or another As Anderson told the *Chicago Tribune* in a 2006 interview:

This funny old series we were doing had a huge influence on the history of television in many ways, from the lighting on television to the kinds of stories that were being told to the characters. The amount of things you see right now where they even just have a male and female as investigators. It's almost a joke. It's like, somebody should come with something

14   Handlen and Vanderwerff. 2018. Monsters of the Week The Complete Critical Companion to *The X-Files*. Abrams Press, p. xviii.

15   Quoted in Tom Shales. 1997. "Fox Americana." *The Washington Post*.

different now![16]

Some of the ways that *The X-Files* influenced television are obvious, and its influence was pointed out by many fans who responded to my questionnaires. As academic Sue Short points out, "*The X-Files* would serve as a landmark in telefantasy by demonstrating that there was a sizeable audience for a contemporary SF/horror show,"[17] and a slew of science-fiction shows were commissioned in its wake. Daniel M. Kimmel, in his history of the Fox network, suggests that the series was copycatted by both CBS (who created the supernatural *American Gothic*) and UPN (which developed the paranoid thriller *Nowhere Man*), while *Dark Skies*, an NBC show that premiered in September 1996, was based on the premise that aliens had been invading Earth since the 1940s and the government was covering it up. *Strange World*, about military investigations into criminal abuses of science and technology, was created by *X-Files* writer Howard Gordon. In September, 2008 Fox premiered the series that was perhaps most influenced by *The X-Files*: *Fringe*, showcasing the work of a division of the FBI that uses fringe science to investigate mysteries related to a parallel universe. *Fringe* creator J. J. Abrams has cited *The X-Files* as a show he'd loved, and executive producer Roberto Orci once noted, "We sat in a room and just listed off our shows. *X-Files* was an inspiration." In addition, blatant references to *The X-Files* appear in the first episode of *Fringe*'s second season: the *X-Files* episode "Dreamland" is playing on the television belonging to a murder victim, and viewers also discover that a previous designation for files similar to those investigated by the *Fringe* team was the letter X. The show's ratings in the first season were lackluster, with some criticizing its similarity to *The X-Files* in the way it featured both monster-of-the-week episodes and a larger narrative, romance between the two leads, and storylines focusing on mind control, astral projection, invisibility,

16   Ryan. 2006. "Gillian Anderson on Lady Dedlock, Dana Scully and the influence of *The X-Files*." *Chicago Tribune*.

17   Short. 2011. *Cult Telefantasy Series: A Critical Analysis of The Prisoner, Twin Peaks, The X-Files, Buffy the Vampire Slayer, Lost, Heroes, Doctor Who and Star Trek* (Vol. 30). McFarland, p. 58.

and genetic mutation. Joshua Alston suggested that the first season of *Fringe* "hewed too closely to *The X-Files*, which was still fresh in the public consciousness thanks to the second theatrical *X-Files* release, *I Want To Believe*." Ratings improved during the show's second season but comparisons with *The X-Files* persisted, especially when Fox moved *Fringe* to 9:00 p.m. on Fridays during season three—the same slot *The X-Files* had occupied in its early days.

The influence of *The X-Files* is visible elsewhere as well. *Lost*, another J. J. Abrams series, developed its own complex mythology and displays what TV scholar Jason Mittell calls "narrative complexity"—an interplay between the demands of episodic and serial storytelling—the prototype for which had its roots in 1980s shows like *Hill Street Blues* and *St. Elsewhere*, though *The X-Files* certainly gave new meaning to the term "complex narrative." The show's influence can also be see in *Torchwood*, developed by *Doctor Who* showrunner Russell T Davies, as well as *Buffy the Vampire Slayer*, which Joss Whedon described as "a cross between *The X-Files* and *My So-Called Life*." Perhaps most significantly, however, the show's writers, directors, and producers have gone on to create numerous critically acclaimed shows, including *Homeland*, developed by Howard Gordon and Alex Gansa; *Supernatural*, directed and produced by Kim Manners; and *Breaking Bad*, created by Vince Gilligan. Carter has said that he is often asked about shows that people think were inspired by *The X-Files*, but for him it's simply that what the show did was tell interesting stories with interesting characters: "I think that if I can take any credit for anything, it's that we were, I think, effective storytellers that had a relentless pursuit of excellence. The thing *The X-Files* did was show that you could tell really scary and suspenseful stories cinematically on network television." Carter didn't have a series bible—a document outlining the story world, characters, plots, and other important elements of the show—and he employed a wide range of writers across the original nine series. While this led to some continuity errors and an increasingly convoluted mytharc, it also allowed the series to play with tone, form, and narrative—giving us the variety of episodes I've discussed throughout this book. Keith Uhlich argues that it's this variety that distinguishes *The X-Files* from other US television series of the time and makes it "something of a bridge between eras, utilizing what came before while developing new narrative and aesthetic approaches that became de rigeur on programs like *Lost* or *Breaking Bad*. Carter provided the template, but his creation allowed for a number of other distinctive voices to emerge. The very unevenness of the show's approach eschewed homogeneity." *Breaking Bad* is undoubtedly one of the success stories of not only *The X-Files*'s writers room but also the second golden age of television. The show played with perspective, style and structure—all areas that Gilligan had developed during his time on *The X-Files*.

Gilligan joined the show as a writer in season two and ended up writing thirty episodes for the original nine seasons. In an interview with the *Huffington Post*, he said, "I learned everything I pretty much know about TV from *The X-Files* and from working for Chris, and from working with Frank Spotnitz and John Shiban." The collaborative nature of the production process, from people "sitting in a room, spitballing" ideas to writers being involved in casting and editing, was an important element. Howard Gordon reflected on this and acknowledged it was a process he used when he went on to develop *24* and *Homeland*:

> I think what was good about *24*, and it has been good about *Homeland*—is the collaboration and the competition. It's a learning experience, and you are protected against your weaknesses by the people around you. It's a wonderful collaborative medium when it's good, and *X-Files* couldn't have been a better grad school. We were all each other's teachers, and I think we all benefited from that combination of collaboration and healthy competition.[18]

Gilligan echoes this sentiment, saying that one thing he learned from Carter was to give the people around him as much investment in the show as possible:

---

18   Ryan. 2013b. "*The X-Files* Anniversary: How Mulder And Scully Led To 'Homeland.'" *Huffington Post*.

When I was a writer on *The X-Files* even before I had a producer title, Chris expected me and the other writers to take responsibility in producing our own episodes. He expected us to go up to Vancouver, in the early days when we still shot up there. He expected us to be available to help the director, to answer any questions, to advocate for the script, to help do all the jobs that a producer does, aide to the director, to the actors, and to the crew in getting the episode produced.[19]

He further says that this experience meant he learned to expect the same from his own writers, and he also points to the visual style of *The X-Files* as an influence on *Breaking Bad*. Carter is often quoted as saying each episode of *The X-Files* was shot as a mini movie, and the show was, in fact, exceptionally cinematic despite appearing on the television screen. The importance of visual storytelling was key to *The X-Files*, and Carter hired talented directors who made the show "visually exciting and interesting"[20] as well as directors of photography like John Bartley and Bill Roe who were able to set the tone for the series and leave the audience with a particular visual from individual episodes that they would remember. Gilligan says he took a lot of those lessons in visual storytelling and "adapted them for use in a show about the gritty and the mundane, a show about the down-and-dirty world of meth dealing. But definitely *Breaking Bad* is a show that's inspired in its look and in its storytelling by *The X-Files*."[21] Frank Spotnitz agrees, noting that writers were expected to suggest visual elements in their scripts and have a sense of how the episode would look on camera, which was unusual in television at the time but is evident among *The X-Files* writers who have gone on to work elsewhere: "That is a thing I think a lot of those guys who graduated from *The X-Files* have in common, they do think visually. They're not

---

19   Ryan 2013a.

20   Cutruzzula. 2013. "Chris Carter on *The X-Files*, His *Sopranos* Jealousy, and Rewriting Vince Gilligan." *Vulture*.

21   Ryan 2013a.

just writing plays to be filmed for television. They really are thinking about how to tell these types of stories with pictures."[22]

XXX

The show's impact on narrative, style and format persists even in the current era, dominated by streaming services, and is recognized by fans and critics as a highly influential series. As one fan who responded to my questionnaire noted, "Since TV has changed so much over the years (less episodes throughout the season, bigger budgets) it made me appreciate and respect the hard work that everyone who made the original series put in all those years ago. They were making ground breaking quality television that is better than a lot of stuff today". This does mean, of course, that the revival seasons also had a lot to live up to. Storytelling has become more complex, production values and budgets are often on a par with those of movies, and the practices that *The X-Files* introduced have become commonplace. For some critics, like Lenika Cruz, the new episodes didn't live up the show's legacy: "It's hard to imagine that *X-Files* newcomers could watch these new episodes and see how a series about two FBI agents with (once) differing world views, and who occasionally brush up against aliens and government conspiracies, could have transformed the history of television."[23]

---

22   Ryan. 2013c. "*The X-Files* Executive Producer Frank Spotnitz On His Biggest Regret And Fondest Memories." *Huffington Post*.

23   Gilbert et al. 2016.

CHAPTER 11

The X-Files Beyond the Small Screen: Transmedia Narratives and Franchise Building

"That's a comic book character my kid Izzy created."
– Shaineh ("Post-Modern Prometheus")

Carter has rejected the idea that *The X-Files* became a mainstream show during season three, telling Brian Lowry, "It was the same dark show—in fact a darker show than it had ever been. It just gained a mainstream audience,"[1] but Fox was savvy in recognizing the market for *The X-Files* beyond the TV show, partly due to its growing audience and partly because of its dedicated fandom. In her article on *The X-Files*'s internet fandom (discussed more in the next chapter), Amanda Howell points out that "print publicity for the series took on the language, rhetoric and concerns of the core Internet fandom of the

---

1   Lowry 1996, p. xvi.

THE TRUTH IS STILL OUT THERE

series in the ritual repetition of lists, FAQs, guides, dossiers, catalogs of episodes and characters, in articles with titles like 'Xcyclopedia' and 'The X-Files from A to X.'"[2] The mid- to late 1990s also saw an increase in the number of official and unofficial books, videos, and other ancillary materials relating to the show, which owed a lot to fan practices like creating character guides, episode listings and publicity archives, and collecting memorabilia. Academic Lincoln Geraghty, in his book on collecting, suggests that certain aspects of the practice are linked to "new and developing technologies associated with video recording, collecting, and the DVD box set,"[3] and for many fans the DVD (or VHS or Blu-ray, depending on their age) was one of the first objects to be added to their collection. That was certainly the case for me with *The X-Files*.

At the beginning of season four, Fox began selling videotapes of "classic" episodes in North America and the United Kingdom. As discussed in the last chapter, the television industry was moving into a new era, defined by changing viewing habits and new technologies, and Fox was able to take advantage of this to expand the reach of the series even farther. Fans of the show had taken to recording episodes on home videocassette recorders, either to rewatch them later or share with fans who may not have been able to catch the episodes when they aired (I still have my VHS tapes, recorded from the BBC in the UK, complete with title and date written in a ring-bound notebook—I was, and still am, a geek). In 1996, though, Fox released the first official VHS tapes in the US and Canada. Each tape, twelve in total, consisted of selected episodes from the first four seasons, including "Pilot"/"Deep Throat," "Duane Barry"/"One Breath," and "Tunguska"/"Terma." The episodes were selected by Carter, and each tape included an introduction by him, explaining why those episodes were chosen and offering anecdotes from the set. A similar process was followed in the UK, with four videos, comprising the first eight

---

2   Howell. 2000. "*The X-Files*, X-Philes and X-Philia: Internet fandom as a site of convergence." *Media International Australia* 97, no. 1, p. 141.

3   Geraghty. 2014. *Cult Collectors*. Routledge, p.56.

episodes of season one, initially being released. These four were the only ones issued in this format, with subsequent videos—or 'files' as they were called—instead featuring two- or three-part episodes edited into feature-length editions. While these included File 2: Tooms ("Squeeze" and "Tooms"), File 3: Abduction ("Duane Barry," "Ascension," and "One Breath"), and File 5: 82517 ("Nisei" and "731"), the first to be released was File 1: The Unopened File. This contained the episodes "Anasazi," "Blessing Way," and "Paperclip," but was released in the UK before the last two episodes had aired on television there—one way to ensure fans who couldn't wait would buy the VHS.

The VHS had been around since the 1970s and offered Fox a way to sell *The X-Files* merchandise to audiences around the globe, but the tapes and later box sets took up a lot of space and were liable to degrade over time. The arrival of the DVD in the late 1990s offered another opportunity to capitalize on the show's success and its dedicated audiences. *The X-Files: The Complete First Season*, released in May 2000, was the first television box set released on DVD and set the tone for what audiences would come to expect as standard. Each season's box set features, in addition to the episodes, audio commentary from producers, directors, and writers; behind-the-scenes shorts; interviews with cast and crew; and other extras. All of these are available via what Derek Kompare calls "evocative animated menus that end in an iconic freeze frame image from the episode chosen to view."[4] The DVD revolutionized the way people watched television. Rather than having to watch shows as they aired, viewers could watch at a time and place that suited them. Of course, this is common for us now—streaming sites like Hulu, Netflix, Amazon Prime, and Disney+ allow us to binge-watch shows as and when we please. And when streaming sites were first introduced, they exposed younger viewers to shows like *The X-Files*, creating a new generation of fans, which played a role in convincing Fox to bring the show back.

When I conducted research with viewers after the revival was announced in 2015, many identified as having been fans for between

---

4   Kompare. 2006. "Publishing Flow: DVD Box Sets and the Reconception of Television." *Television & New Media*, 7(4), p. 348.

zero and ten years and coming to the show because of its inclusion in streaming platforms like Netflix. Some of these had known of the show before they started watching, like the fan who said it had been in their Netflix queue for a while but they knew they'd be obsessed with it and needed to spend their time on classes, not TV. Others were introduced to the show because their parents or family members had been fans when the series originally aired, like this fan:

> I began watching the show in late December 2011 at the age of 15 (I'm 18 now). Both of my parents are fans, but my dad is a huge X-Phile and inspired me to watch the show. It has been one of my favorite shows of all time ever since.

Fox used this new interest in the series, the passion of older fans, and the emergence of social networking sites like Snapchat and Twitter to hype up season ten. During the production and release of *I Want to Believe*, the network officialized the fan site X-Files News (XFN) and granted its volunteers access to cast, crew, and the red-carpet premiere. Fox worked with XFN during the revival seasons, but it also ran a series of social media campaigns, including a #thexfiles201days rewatch hosted on Twitter that encouraged fans to watch the show on streaming sites in order to take part. Much as the DVD box sets had offered fans behind-the-scenes features and a different perspective on the themes underpinning and decisions behind each season, the Fox social media activity allowed the audience to see a different perspective on the show's legacy and its return. To launch the rewatch, Fox posted a custom video including both old and new footage, and throughout the campaign, Duchovny, Anderson, and Mitch Pileggi conducted live Q & As during specific episodes. Fox also ran a #FindTheX campaign on Twitter, which sent fans on a scavenger hunt to unlock exclusive content about the upcoming season. The show's official Twitter account would post a tweet suggesting a link to a character, played by an actor who was also on Twitter. Fans would then visit that actor's profile, where they would be encouraged to retweet the #FindTheX post until it had reached a predetermined number of retweets set by Fox. Once the number was reached, the official *X-Files* account would

post a link to a Tumblr page and a password to access it—accessing
the page allowed fans to watch exclusive content. As academics
Daiana Sigiliano and Gabriela Borges note, however, fan engagement
didn't stop with watching the content: fans broke down the videos
they had watched into frames and analyzed these in an attempt to
uncover more details about the upcoming season. One video, which
featured the silhouette of a man smoking, led fans to conclude that
Cigarette Smoking Man would be featured in season ten despite
having been killed off in season nine, while another offered some hints
about William, the child Scully gave up for adoption in season nine.
Sigiliano and Borges break this down, writing "After analyzing the
videos shared by Find The X, the fan discovered a frame in which the
character calls his biological parents. This led to further analysis: using
screen captures from Fox's transmedia strategy, interacting fandom
compared Mulder's and Scully's hands to figure out who had received
William's phone call."[5] While Fox's strategy worked in attracting both
new and return viewers to season ten, it also offered hints and clues to
engaged fans who had the time and resources to analyze the published
videos. In this respect, the season ten campaign drew on tactics Fox
had previously used to take *The X-Files* beyond television by leveraging
transmedia storytelling.

XXX

In simple terms, transmedia storytelling is telling stories across
multiple media, so that each medium can do what it does best. Henry
Jenkins offers the following explanation: "A story might be introduced
in a film, expanded through television, novels, and comics, and its
world might be explored and experienced through game play."[6] Each
of these applies to *The X-Files*. The TV show had already introduced
the concept of mytharc and monster-of-the-week episodes, a format

---

5   Sigiliano and Borges. 2019. "Transmedia literacy: Analyzing the impact of *The X-Files* transmedia
     strategies." *Palabra Clave*, 22(2), p. 18.

6   Jenkins. 2006. *Convergence Culture: Where Old and New Media Collide*. NYU Press, p.95.

that worked well (at least until the mytharc became unruly in the later seasons of the original run), and expanding this into different media made sense. In 1994, Fox branched into print with the publication of *Goblins*, the first of six original novels set in *The X-Files* universe. This was followed the next year by two other original novels and *X Marks the Spot*—the first in a series of book adaptations of episodes aimed at a younger audience. In total, thirty novelizations were published, in addition to six original novels and a series of comic books. While the novelizations attempted to introduce a younger audience to the show by offering simpler versions of the episodes, the original novels and the comic books offered the opportunity to explore aspects of the *X-Files* universe that didn't fit the TV format. Writer Kevin J Anderson, who wrote three of the original novels, recalled Carter telling him, "'As a writer you have an unlimited special effects budget, and so write a story that we could never afford to film as a TV episode,' and I went, 'That's really cool cos I could blow things up all over the place.'"[7] Anderson's novel *Ruins* allowed Mulder and Scully to investigate beyond the confines of the US, flying to the Yucatan jungle to investigate the disappearance of a team of archaeologists, but he points out that each novel had to be approved by Carter and a team at Ten Thirteen to ensure it aligned with the overarching themes of the show and the characterizations of Mulder and Scully.

This process was also implemented with the books that coincided with *The X-Files* revival. A year before season ten aired, IDW Publishing produced the first of three short-story anthologies featuring stories about *The X-Files*, the others following in 2016. Authorized by Carter and edited by Jonathan Maberry, the collections included stories from Kevin J. Anderson and Joe Harris, who had both written previous works for the franchise (Anderson's offering had in fact been approved by Carter years earlier but had never been used). In 2017, an authorized prequel series was published. *The X-Files Origins* comprised two books depicting Mulder and Scully at the ages of seventeen and fifteen during the spring of 1979. With the occult, serial murder, and government

---

7   The X-Cast: An *X-Files* Podcast. 2021. "521. Interview: Kevin J. Anderson (author of *Ground Zero, Ruins & Antibodies*)."

conspiracies in the news, the series follows Mulder and Scully as they experience life-changing events that set them on the path to the X-Files. Although these were targeted at teenagers, Jonathan Maberry, who wrote the Scully-centric *Devil's Advocate*, hoped to reach a wider audience, saying he wrote them "for anyone who loves a good mystery and who also loves *The X-Files*. We're hoping that the *X-Files* fan base enjoys the book as much as we do but at the same time a new audience reads the books and then watches the show. I mean, there are a lot of teens who haven't watched *X-Files*, and we know they're missing out. We want them to watch the show and have as much fun as we did."[8] Considering the issues involved when using a more transmedia approach to a franchise, Kami Garcia, who wrote the Mulder-focused *Agents of Chaos*, said, "I want Mulder to feel real. I don't want people to be like, 'Oh, I'm reading a book about a character in a television show.' To true fans, the characters you love almost feel like real people, and I especially don't want fans to come back and be like, 'Ugh, this is a disappointing read.'"[9] Fox has continued its transmedia approach in print, publishing *The X-Files: The Official Archives—Cryptids, Biological Anomalies, and Parapsychic Phenomena* in 2020. Offering an illustrated look into fifty of the show's monster-of-the-week episodes, the book exists within the world of *The X-Files* as the reader "becomes" Agent Leyla Harrison, who is helping Skinner archive the X-Files. The book includes field reports, newspaper clippings, and photographs as well as handwritten notes by Harrison answering some of the questions about what had happened on the cases Mulder and Scully had investigated.

The X-Files has appeared in comic form as well. The first of these were published by Topps comics between 1995 and 1998 and followed a similar structure to the show, with writer/artist team Stephen Petrucha and Charlie Adlard creating a combination of monster-of-the-week and serialized-narrative issues set between seasons two

8   Longo. 2017a. "*X-Files Origins*: Author Jonathan Maberry on Young Dana Scully's Path To Belief." *Den of Geek*.

9   Longo. 2017b. "*X-Files Origins*: Inside The Mind of Young Fox Mulder With Author Kami Garcia." *Den of Geek*.

and five. According to Petrucha in an afterword to the first comic, several companies were in the running for the comic book rights, demonstrating just how popular the series had become.[10] Fans also responded positively to the first issue; the letters page in issue two commented on how Adlard had captured the mood of *The X-Files* and suggested the comics might appeal to readers who had yet to watch the show. It seemed that Fox's attempts to attract a new audience through a transmedia approach was working. Writing about the making of *The X-Files* comic book series, Topps editor Dwight Jon Zimmerman confirmed that attracting a new audience had always been one of the aims: "Our goal was to create a great comic book that could stand on its own, regardless of whether you ever watched *The X-Files* or not,"[11] and recruiting established writers and artists was one way to introduce new readers to the show. As licensed properties, the comics featured the text "created by Chris Carter" on their front covers and were subject to the same approvals as the books. Discussing Topps Issue #7, "Trepanning Opera," however, academic Nicolas Pillai points out that comics aren't always beholden to the license holders and can be more subversive in their narrative storytelling. In the final frames of the comic, an ambiguous sketch shows Scully falling from darkness into light. The suggestion is that Scully, rather than the villain of the story, may have plummeted to her death and, as Petrucha notes, Fox/ Ten Thirteen wanted the sequence cut:

> Incidentally, we had a *huge* fight with Ten Thirteen over the ending. They absolutely wanted it cut out, afraid that readers would think Scully had actually died—an issue which strikes me, to this day, as absolutely ridiculous. If anything, the readers were *the* audience to understand it was a question mark about reality in general, and Scully would be back next issue or episode or whatever. The original caption, more to the point, was "How do you know you didn't die?" I changed it

---

10   Petrucha. 1994. "Welcome to *The X-Files* Comic." *The X-Files Issue #1*, p. 30.

11   Zimmerman. 1995. "The Making of *The X-Files* Comic Book Series." *The X-Files Issue #0*, p. 47.

to the weaker "You may only be imagining that you survived." But I think they *still* wanted it pulled. Of course the story dies without it. I seem to remember Topps Comics running the ending without their approval. It was only one in a long line of problems trying to do the book, which ultimately led to my dismissal, but aesthetically it was the most frustrating[12]

The response from readers published in the issue letters page of the following issue was overwhelmingly positive and didn't suggest that fans thought Scully had actually died. Yet this demonstrates some of the tensions at work in developing a transmedia narrative. A second set of comics was published by WildStorm Comics between 2008 and 2009, these written by Frank Spotnitz, who also cowrote *I Want to Believe*, the 2008 *X-Files* film. Although the comics and the movie shared the same name, they were substantially different; the comics are set within the narrative continuity of seasons two to five of the original show. This allowed Spotnitz to use characters who were no longer part of the series by the time the film was produced and ignore potential issues of continuity:

> It would have been too restricted and complicated. There were many things about Mulder and Scully's lives that we deliberately left oblique in the last movie, and I wasn't eager to spell them out in the comic book world. It seemed like it would be more fun—and open up more storytelling possibilities—to set the comics "out of time," in an unspecified era of the TV series, roughly between seasons three and five.[13]

While the Topps comics place Carter front and center on the cover, the WildStorm comics feature only the names of the writer and artist. The first thing we see inside, however, is an artistic rendering of the

12 Pillai. 2013. "'What am I looking at, Mulder?': Licensed comics and the freedoms of transmedia storytelling." *Science Fiction Film and Television*, 6(1), pp. 110-111.

13 Pillai 2013 p. 113.

show's title sequence spread over six frames, with the text "created by Chris Carter" to the very right of the final frame in the same place as it sits in the show's opening sequence. For Pillai, "these 'title sequences' encapsulate the transmedia project of the licensed comic, reminding us of the television programme but establishing formal distance from it."[14] Yet references to earlier episodes are peppered through the comics: one panel in *Issue #0* shows us the final issue of "The Great Mutato" comic book introduced in season five's "Post-Modern Prometheus," while *Issue #1* shows Skinner watching a weather report presented by Holman Hardt—better known for controlling the weather in season six's "Rain King."

Following the poor performance of *I Want to Believe*, which seemed to bring to an end the idea that the franchise might continue with another film, Carter returned to comics. In an interview published in 2008's *Issue #0*, he acknowledges that "*The X-Files* has proven to be such a flexible concept. It's allowed us to showcase the talents of so many writers; the comic book is an opportunity to expand on that,"[15] and producing another series with IDW Publishing offered an opportunity for *The X-Files* to return in a way that could expand the TV narrative. But unlike the earlier comics, which had been set in a timeline adjacent to the original nine seasons, these comics would be set in the present day and form a canonical season ten and eleven.[16] Published by IDW between 2013 and 2015, the comics opened with Mulder and Scully living together in "peaceful anonymity" under the name Blake. Carter was announced as executive producer for the comics, with his name appearing first on the covers, before those of writer Joe Harris, artist Michael Walsh, and colorist Jordie Bellaire, and the comics were considered a canonical extension of the TV series.

---

14   Ibid.

15   Carter. 2008. "A Word With Chris Carter." *The X-Files #0*, p. 43.

16   Various crossover comics were also created, demonstrating the series could exist in multiple different universes across multiple different genres. *The X-Files/30 Days of Night* series was published in 2011; *The X-Files/Ghostbusters: Conspiracy*, *The X-Files/Teenage Mutant Ninja Turtles: Conspiracy*, *The X-Files/The Crow: Conspiracy* and *The X-Files/Transformers: Conspiracy* following in 2014. In 2017 a comic featuring the Funko! Pop figure versions of Mulder and Scully was published, tying in with the physical Funko! Pop merchandise.

Of course, we know now that the show would return to TV only a few years after the comic season eleven was published, rendering the comics noncanon, but these and other print versions of *The X-Files* show just how well a franchise can work off-screen and the different impacts that a transmedia narrative can have.

XXX

Fox also created transmedia storylines on screen, however. In addition to the television series, two films were produced as well as the spinoff series *The Lone Gunmen*, and *Millennium*, which included a crossover episode in season seven of *The X-Files*. The franchise also appeared on the computer screen, with Fox developing three video games based on the series: *The X-Files: Unrestricted Access* (1997), *The X-Files Game* (1998), and *The X-Files: Resist or Serve* (2004).[17] *The X-Files: Unrestricted Access* was less a computer game and more an interactive database offering players information from the show's first four seasons. Produced by Fox Interactive, working closely with Carter, the game suggests that the player has hacked into a highly classified secret government website within which you explore case files, examine evidence in 3D and view "live" surveillance footage of Mulder's and Scully's homes and office. Although *The X-Files: Unrestricted Access* doesn't extend the narrative of the show, it does allow players access to a deeper understanding.

The 1999 *X-Files Game*, set during the third season of the TV show, takes a different approach. Using a point-and-click interface that allows the player to explore different aspects of the X-Files, the game introduces Special Agent Craig Willmore, who is assigned by Skinner to investigate the disappearances of Mulder and Scully. The game, written by Richard Dowdy, Greg Roach, and Frank Spotnitz, based on a story by Carter and Spotnitz, gives players the opportunity to interact with other characters through multiple options from which players can choose. Although the game features a number of cut scenes

---

17   A fourth game, *The X-Files: Deep State*, was published in 2018 for iOS, Android and Facebook.

and involved show's actors, it has never been considered a part of the show's canon. In fact, some academics have asked whether it's a game or if it should be considered an "interactive movie."[18] Rather than simply watching an episode, with no control over its outcome, game players are able to perform a range of actions both "right" and "wrong." Pointing a gun at a colleague, for example, results in them telling you not to do that; shooting them sees your mug shot being taken before you go to jail (and ending the game); shooting the wall instead leads to a reprimand, and you are forced to relinquish your badge. In addition to being able to choose actions, players can select different emotional responses from a set of icons that appear on the screen and subtly affect the narrative flow. Selecting "mean" when responding to Agent Cook, for example, means the agent may not cover you as he should later in the game. The game was received positively, but one key criticism involved the decision to use an original character as the playable protagonist rather than Mulder or Scully. As Stephen Jacobs, Geoffery Long, Kathering Isbister and Richard Rouse III point out, "This may have been, in some ways, a win for the TV show's IP holders, but it was a frustration for some players."[19] The game didn't sell as well as expected, failing to attract enough of the show's TV audience.

XXX

The final video game in the franchise, and the one that perhaps epitomized Fox's transmedia strategy following the end of the series, was *The X-Files: Resist or Serve*, set during the show's seventh season and released two years after the series had ended. According to Jason Mittell, one of the goals of television's transmedia strategies is to sustain audience's interest during breaks. The earlier video games, and many of the books and comics, had been published while the series was on the

---

18   Perron, Bernard, Arsenault, Picard, and Therrien. 2008. "Methodological questions in 'interactive film studies.'" *New Review of Film and Television Studies* 6, (3), pp.233-252.

19   Jacobs, Long, Isbister, and Rouse III. 2006. "Occasionally reconcilable differences: bringing games and linear entertainment IP together, for better and for worse." *In Proceedings of the 2006 ACM SIGGRAPH symposium on Videogames*, p. 13.

air, fulfilling both Fox's goal of providing an additional revenue stream while driving viewers back to the television series and Carter's aim of supporting and strengthening the core television narrative experience.[20] *Resist or Serve*, however, much like the season ten and eleven comics, was designed to keep *The X-Files* in the public consciousness while the show was off the air and reward loyal audiences who wanted to see more of Mulder and Scully. The game itself was set after "The Sixth Extinction II: Amor Fati" and was advertised as comprising three "lost" episodes from the seventh season. These episodes made up the three levels of the survival/horror-style game, which can be played as either Mulder or Scully and requires you to solve puzzles, kill enemies, and occasionally perform an autopsy. Associate producer and storyboard artist Ben Borth said, "We wanted to present more of a classic 'X-Files' game experience,"[21] adding that "being written by one of the writers from the show [Thomas Schnauz, who wrote seasons nine's "Lord of the Flies" and "Scary Monsters"], it brings a true 'X-Files' story into an interactive experience and combines with it the well-developed and well-known characters from the series."[22] Indeed, while gameplay was criticized, the game's appeal to fans and the ways in which developer Black Ops Entertainment achieved that were pointed out by all of its reviewers.

Fox's attempts at transmedia storytelling might have been more successful in some mediums than in others, but they nevertheless show that the franchise was able to exist—and succeed—beyond the screen. Fans who engaged with all of the mediums were also able to deepen their understanding of and appreciation for the TV series, with one fan, talking about season ten, saying "I thought it was an interesting way to recover a lot of the loose storylines from the series, comics, and movies while still sticking to the original vision for the show." Fans are aware of the aspects of the show that exist beyond the screen—although only 265 of the 862 fans who responded to

---

20   Mittell 2015, p. 295.

21   Lipsey. 2004. "New PS2 game allows fans another fling with their favorite 'X'." *CNN.com*.

22   Von Kallenbach. 2004. *Skiewed and Reviewed 2004 Back for More*, p. 209.

my pre-season ten questionnaire had read the comics, the bulk of those who answered "no" had heard of them—and in some cases the revival seasons encouraged fans to revisit the comics and other tie-in media. Fans were also aware of the possibilities for extending the story world should season eleven be the final television installment, with one acknowledging that "we have the comics [and] whatever other properties continue the stories." And of course fans also have unofficial transmedia narratives like fan videos, fan art, and fan fiction (discussed in Chapter Eight) through which they can extend the storyline and keep *The X-Files* alive.

CHAPTER 12

The Fandom Is Out There

*"We're all hopping on the internet to nitpick the scientific inaccuracies of **Earth 2**."*

—Langly ("One Breath")

I've referred to the internet and various fan activities throughout the course of this book, but I want to take a closer look at the fandom in this chapter. In many ways, the history of *The X-Files* is closely linked with the history of the fandom—and indeed, fandom more widely: just as the series influenced the TV shows that came after it, so has its fandom influenced the fandoms that followed. Terms like "shipping" that are commonly used in fandoms from *Doctor Who* to K-pop originated with *The X-Files*,[1] as did the popularization of show- and fandom-specific acronyms,[2] while the fandom also advocated for the ability to reuse, adapt, and share aspects of the show under the US's "fair use" laws, following attempts by Fox to curb this kind of

---

1   Romano. 2016. "Canon, fanon, shipping and more: a glossary of the tricky terminology that makes up fan culture." *Vox.*

2   Alp. 2021. "How *The X-Files* Shaped Online Fandom Culture As We Know It." *Medium.*

fan activity.[3] It's easy to forget, with smartphones, social media sites, and access to fellow fans, actors, and producers at your fingertips, how revolutionary the internet was in the early nineties. Growing up in the UK, I didn't have the internet at home until I was in my late teens, though I do remember that the first time I ever went online, I immediately headed to AOL to look for fellow X-Philes. The name for *X-Files* fans, derived from the Greek word *philos*, which means "to love," was an appropriate one for a group of young, highly educated, technologically adept viewers who wanted to discuss the series with like-minded viewers.

Philes are often considered to be among the first fan groups to develop virtual fan cultures online. Created on the Usenet newsgroup in December 1993, alt.tv.x-files was one of the first *X-Files* online fan sites. Posts made to the group on its first day discussed Mulder's mysterious informant Deep Throat, nitpicked over Scully's medical diploma,[4] and analyzed the show's standing in the Neilson ratings, among other things. Brian Lowry, author of *The Official Guide to The X-Files*, suggests that "fan reaction to the series has become as much a part of *The X-Files* story as the show itself, from the conventions that have sprung up around the country to the hours of chat about the series whipping around each week on the Internet."[5] Reeves, Rogers, and Epstein have noted that fans of the show maintained (and, I would argue, continue to maintain) a "high profile on the express lane of the information superhighway." Fans created a presence for the show online even before Fox did; by the time the official website had been created in June 1995, scores of unofficial websites and message boards had already appeared. As Bambi Haggins notes, the unofficial fan clubs remained grassroots fan organizations after the Official Fan Club was created, and *The X-Files* fan pages arguably set the standard

---

3   Allair. 2018. "*The X-Files*: A History of the Fandom." *Den of Geek*.

4   Carter has acknowledged that in the early days of the show at least, he regularly interacted with fans online, although the critical dissection of the show by some fans drove him mad at times. Possibly the inspiration for Langly's line in season two's "One Breath" that appears at the start of this chapter.

5   Lowry 1995, p. 239.

for impressive sites of fandom:

> . . . for lustful chatting and sophisticated star worship, see
> David Duchovny Estrogen Brigade website brought to you
> by Sarah Steagall et al; for the perusal of extensive archival
> notes, see Cliff Chen's slightly dated but extremely thorough
> X-Files FAQ', for a taste of wryly humorous X-Files dialogue,
> see over fifty online list of "Mulderisms & Scullyisms"; and
> to post messages to other X-Philes, see alt.tv.x-files, which,
> even in this post-series era, remains an active space for online
> discourse.[6]

Malinda Lo points out that it wasn't until season seven that the
official website began to offer "anything approaching the content
of fan websites."[7] Fox decided to make further investments in the
site in order to "beat the fan websites at their game by providing
news, episode summaries, and insider information to fans that was
unavailable elsewhere on the web,"[8] and the official website did
become the place to go to for online chats with Carter, Duchovny,
and Anderson. This engagement between fans and producers seemed
to suggest more possibilities for interaction, and Carter has recognized
that the growth of the internet came at a good time for the growth
of the show, saying the internet was like an "interactive tool" helping
him measure the "pulse" of the audience.[9] Frank Spotnitz remembers
going online during the early days of show's second season:

> A lot of writers were reluctant to see what the fans were
> writing, but I was always curious to see how the show was
> being received. I only browsed and never contributed to the

6   Haggins. 2002. "Apocrypha Meets the Pentagon Papers: The Appeals of *The X-Files* to the X-Phile."
    Journal of Film and Video 53:4, p. 12.

7   Lo. 2001. "Building *The X-Files*: Television Production, Authorship, and Discourse." *Malinda Lo.*.

8   Ibid.

9   Haggins 2002, p. 13.

forums, but it was extremely useful to see how the episodes were playing—what fans liked, what they didn't like, and where they thought the show was going.[10]

Haggins suggests that the producers' interest in what fans thought seemed to herald a new age of interactivity between the two sides of the screen, and the ongoing story arc was indeed influenced by fans, as Spotnitz notes:

> I remember one specific instance where I was actually inspired to write an episode because of something I read on a message board. It was during the third season, and I was flying back from a fan convention in Minnesota when I read one comment noting that we hadn't followed up on the death of Scully's sister earlier in the year. I realized that this was not only true, but an enormous oversight. I thought about it all the way to the airport, and by the time my plane landed in Los Angeles, I'd outlined most of the episode that became "Piper Maru."[11]

By frequenting fan forums and allowing fan opinion to shape the storylines, *The X-Files*'s writers and producers openly embraced their fans, and that recognition of the fans became a part of the show through the use of their names in the opening sequences of season nine. Each opening sequence during the show's final season highlighted the online monikers of fans and, as Bertha Chin suggests, was intended as a public thank you note from the producers. The appearance of Special Agent Leyla Harrison in season eight's "Alone" demonstrates another way in which fans were recognized: the character was named in honor of an *X-Files* fan fiction writer who had died in 2001 after a two-year battle with cancer.

---

10   Jones. 2013a. "The Fandom Is Out There: Social Media and *The X-Files* Online" in Kristin M. Barton and Jonathan Malcolm Lampley (eds) *Fan CULTure: Essays on participatory fandom in the 21st century*. McFarland p. 94.

11   Ibid p. 95.

XXX

In addition to alt.tv.x-files, other Usenet groups and mailing lists sprung up in the early years of the show, among them alt.tv.x-files. creative and Yes Virginia for fan fiction writers; the David Duchovny Estrogen Brigade and Gillian Anderson Testosterone Brigade, which focus on the show's stars; and a plethora of character-related groups, including RATales (dedicated to Krycek), Skinner Fans, and Black Lung Association (for discussion related to Cigarette Smoking Man). This wealth of internet discussion proved extremely useful in promoting the series and continued following the show's end after season nine. The emergence of social networking sites such as Facebook and Twitter provides fans with new ways of communicating with both other fans and producers, and fans adopted these technologies as easily as their predecessors had adopted Usenet and AOL.

Henry Jenkins argues that web 2.0 has changed the proximity fans have to media producers, who also make use of social networks and blogs to communicate with fans either directly or via an assistant who writes the blogs or tweets on their behalf. David Duchovny briefly blogged about filming *I Want to Believe* in a blog set up by Fox, and Spotnitz maintained a blog through his production company, Big Light Productions, which he considers "less a blog than a conversation."[12] Spotnitz's blog also played host to a social network for fans. Discussing the decision to host such a network, he says:

> I didn't really know where this would lead—I just thought it was a unique opportunity to connect with fans and see what they were thinking. Since that time, my relationship with the fans has grown much closer. We have an ongoing dialogue and I know many of them by name.[13]

Through the blog, Spotnitz arranged for fans to be able to attend the

---

12   Jones 2013a, p. 95.

13   Ibid p. 96.

2008 premieres of *I Want to Believe* in Los Angeles and London, and he continued to give fans information on timings and schedules of promotional events related to the film. He also began to get a sense of the people communicating with him through the blog: "a group of frequent correspondents [. . .] emerged so I started to get a sense of who the people were who were most frequently on the social network [. . .] then you started to get a sense of their personalities and their sense of humor and it's all over the world, from Australia to Europe to the Middle East to Russia [. . .] I can tell you about *X-Files* fans now on every continent."[14] And fans do exist on every continent. Respondents to the questionnaires I circulated came from the US, Argentina, Turkey, India, Costa Rica, Malaysia, and many other countries, with some having been fans since the series first aired and others coming to the fandom only within the previous five years. The global spread of *The X-Files* fandom was evident in a fan campaign run by X-Files News (XFN), an *X-Files* fan site created in October 2007.

Originally set up to promote *I Want to Believe*, it was officialized by Fox in mid-2008—the only fan site to be granted that honor and the only fansite on the red carpet for the LA premiere of the film. As a thank you to the cast and crew and a celebration of the fandom, XFN created "Place," a nine-minute video that featured Philes from twenty-six countries saying, "Where I'm from it's always Ten Thirteen."[15] Fan activities didn't stop there. In the spring of 2009, XFN attended a book signing by Carter and asked what fans could do to convince Fox to greenlight a third feature film. Carter suggested that fans should write letters to Fox, stating that this approach had worked for the second movie. The XF3 Army Campaign: Believe in the Future was launched, which consisted of XFN collecting fan-made postcards showing images from the series sent in from across the globe; the creation of poster and trailers for a third film; and a "10,013 photos

---

14   Ibid.

15   The video is available on YouTube at https://www.youtube.com/watch?v=Ntc3ZYlmdvs. Full disclosure: I am in that video, along with a group of friends I met through the fandom and with whom I went on the attend the 2008 London premiere and multiple 'Philemunes' where we rewatched our favorite episodes of the show. The clip we sent in was recorded at one of those.

for a green-light" campaign in April 2011. XFN has also used social media to raise awareness of the show, especially through Twitter. Its first Twitter campaign began on September 10, 2011, after a fan approached XFN and asked if it would consider launching a campaign to celebrate eighteen years since *The X-Files* first premiered. It did, and almost 17,000 tweets containing the hashtag XF3 were sent to Fox, with actors Annabeth Gish and BD Wong, who guest starred in season three's "Hell Money," also throwing their support behind the campaign. The second took place on October 13, 2011, to celebrate Carter's birthday, and by the end of the campaign, over 32,000 tweets had been sent. A third campaign, designed to get *X-Files*-related hashtags trending in order to lobby for a third film, ran in 2012. The tweet-a-thon took place across multiple time zones, running from the moment the first time zone (New Zealand) hit midnight on March10 until the last time zone (Hawaii) hit midnight on March 11, and the #txf3 hashtag ended up trending fifth worldwide.

The various XFN campaigns, and the fans who took part in them, clearly demonstrated that the fandom still existed and that there was a desire to see the franchise continue in some format. Fox was aware of these campaigns and fans' continued interest in the franchise; a source at the studio described XFN as being "surprisingly consistent and well organized,"[16] and a few years later, fans were once again taking to social media to call for the studio to reprise the show. In a January 2015 interview with the Nerdist podcast, Anderson confirmed that she would be up for returning to the show and asked the hosts if they thought Fox should do anything in their power to make it happen. The resulting discussion led to the creation of the #xfiles2015 hashtag, with Nerdist host Chris Hardwick telling listeners, "Simply tweet all your #XFiles2015 feelings to Fox for your chance to be heard. We want to believe."[17] Fans responded to that call, with one telling me, "I was ecstatic but I didn't believe anything would come of it. Once #xfiles2015 started happening due to Gillian Anderson being on the

---

16   Munn. 2011. "Tiffany Devol Talks About XF3 Campaign: 'We Were Blown Away.'" *Suite 101*.

17   *The Nerdist Podcast*. 2015. "The Nerdist Podcast Number 623: Gillian Anderson."

Nerdist… let's just say I was hash tagging everything." Later that month, Fox confirmed it was in the "logistical" stage of planning for the franchise's return.

Clearly it would be wrong to say that fans were responsible for significantly shaping episodes and storylines or for reviving the show.[18] As academic Derek Johnson points out, "We must not uncritically accept this shift [in the relationship among audiences, texts, and institutions of production] as evidence of growing audience power."[19] Spotnitz agrees with this, suggesting that while perceptions of fans have changed and "there's so much two-way communication now through websites, through Facebook, through Twitter, that people are much more aware these are not crazy people, they're passionate people,"[20] studios realize the vocal fans are only a small percentage of the overall audience. Of course, Fox was aware of *The X-Files* fan base and used it to encourage both returning and new viewers to watch season ten, and looking at the history of *The X-Files* fandom, it is difficult to separate the show from the fandom and its influence.

XXX

The fandom that began around the show has developed over the years into taking action in the real world as well. X-Files News (XFN) had already established itself as a source for fandom news and had run a series of campaigns after the release of *I Want to Believe* designed to convince Fox to greenlight a third film. It also branched out into charity work with a What Would Frankenbear Do? Worldwide Tour. The campaign was created by XFN in association with the Skype Files

18 Anderson did reveal at Dallas Comic Con in June 2015 that when she was on the Nerdist podcast, they were already in the middle of negotiations with Fox to bring *The X-Files* back, and asking about a revival and creating a hashtag was a "clever way to get a grassroots movement going to rally the troops" (Wallace. 2015. "10 Things We Learned From Gillian Anderson's Dallas Comic Con Panel." *The Nerdist*.

19 Johnson. 2007. "Inviting audiences in: The spatial reorganization of production and consumption in 'TVIII'." *New Review of Film and Television Studies*, 5 (1), p. 73.

20 Jones 2013a, p. 103.

and IBG, Inc., two other fandom organizations. The idea behind the campaign was that a stuffed teddy bear called Frankenbear (named after Frank Spotnitz) would travel the globe while raising money for the UCLA-Santa Monica Rape Treatment Center. X-Philes from around the world took turns hosting Frankenbear, taking him on sightseeing tours of their cities and uploading pictures with him to XFN and a range of social networking sites before sending him on to his next "family." I spent a week in London with a group of friends I had met through *The X-Files* fandom, including Philes from the US and Australia who had traveled to the UK. During the week we hosted Frankenbear and took him with us to attractions such as the Tower of London, Buckingham Palace, and the London Eye as well as on a boat trip down the Thames before sending him off to his next hosts along with souvenirs that were included in the packages, such as badges and items of clothing. We uploaded photographs that we took during Frankenbear's stay to our personal Facebook pages and sent them to XFN, which was blogging about the campaign for its duration and managing Frankenbear's Big Light profile page, where "he" was providing an account of the trip. In total Frankenbear traveled to twenty-five countries and stayed with dozens of fans. Discussing the campaign, XFN's Avi Quijada wrote:

> Inspired by the kindness of his namesake, after a trip 9 months long, and visiting over 20 different countries and hundreds of *X-Files* Fans, Frankenbear managed to create a community experience that allowed Philes from over the world to share a sentiment that conquered distances. As a final perk of this feat, Frankenbear also raised awareness and gathered donations for the UCLA-Santa Monica Rape Treatment Center.[21]

Indeed, almost $1,500 was sent to the UCLA-Santa Monica Rape Treatment Center. XFN wasn't the only fan group that did charitable work in the name of *The X-Files*, however. Aussie *X-Files* Fans @

21   Jones 2013a, p. 99.

Facebook (AXF) and heART for Charity both carried out fundraising events and undertook charity work inspired by Gillian Anderson through their fandom of *The X-Files*.

AXF was established as a Facebook group by Sandi Hicks after she realized there was no Australian fan base for the show on the platform. At the beginning, she had no plans to undertake any charitable work; it was intended to be a space where fans could discuss the show and the then-forthcoming second film. The idea to raise money came when Gillian Anderson announced she was expecting her third child:

> I thought it would be nice for us to throw together a small fundraiser as a present for her, rather than send her a whole heap of baby goods that she would probably neither want or need – or to send her flowers that would just die.[22]

Sandi raised funds by selling Aussie X-Philes T-shirts, holding *X-Files* episode marathons at which groups of fans met up to watch *X-Files* episodes and donate money, and auctioning autographed memorabilia donated by Anderson on eBay. The first fundraiser raised AU $2,036.04, which was sent to Alinyiikira Junior School—an organization that Anderson supports—and the fans received a message of thanks from Anderson for both the donations and a book that Sandi had compiled containing photographs of fans who had donated, a short biography, and favorite *X-Files* quotes and episodes. The message spurred Sandi to continue fundraising for the school, creating an annual event that increasingly saw more *X-Files* alumni, including Chris Carter, Frank Spotnitz, David Duchovny, and William B. Davis, contributing items for eBay auctions. In total, AXF raised close to AU $20,000 for Alinyiikira Junior School, and while the fundraising was influenced by Anderson's philanthropy, it was only through *The X-Files* and the character of Scully that Sandi and her fellow fans became aware of the actress.

heART for Charity's impetus for fundraising came from a slightly

---

22   Jones 2012.

different angle. Founder Roxane B was inspired to set up the group in June 2008 after attending a "Scully Marathon" in Paris, a fan event held to raise funds for charities by auctioning off rare *X-Files* merchandise and other related collectibles to fans. As an art student in France, Roxane recognized the charitable potential of her Gillian Anderson-inspired artwork. The following years, she appealed to other *X-Files* and Gillian Anderson fans who were sharing their artwork online and recruited thirteen artists from Italy, The Netherlands, the US, France, Taiwan, the UK, Poland, Germany, and South Korea to create and auction off their art. Roxane and fellow artist SG developed a name, logo, and website, and spent several months preparing for the auctions and obtaining official clearance from Anderson as well as the charity they had chosen to support. The crux of the project was two weeks of online auctions in June 2010. Using eBay's charity branch, MissionFish, heART auctioned off fourteen original artworks and raised £650 for Off the Street Kids—a charity aiding the empowerment of marginalized children and young people in South Africa. Unlike those at AXF, the artists involved in this fundraising emphasized the impact that *The X-Files*, rather than Anderson, had on them. One artist, Scooly, noted that she loves Gillian's acting, but "I'm a fan of her show rather than specifically her. I would participate if it was David's, Chris', Frank's or really anyone's, I suppose. I just wanted to draw a nice *X-Files* pic and see if someone would buy it to help some kids." What was particularly interesting in talking to fans was the way that the message of the show led them to thinking about making changes in the real world. One fan told me:

Being a part of *The X-Files* community and knowing that Gillian Anderson personally endorses various charities is inspiring in itself. Furthermore, the general message in *The X-Files* of "not giving up" and "what can be imagined can be achieved" is especially pertinent seeing as these fundraisers are directed towards *The X-Files* fans. It goes to show how applicable the messages in the show are to the causes that the group supports.[23]

And fans of *The X-Files* continue to create and contribute to projects inspired by the show. In 2018, Carly Blake and Lauren Krattiger decided to partner up for the *X-Files* Fan Retrospective project, interviewing over ninety cast and crew members and dozens of fans about *The X-Files* and how it had shaped their lives ahead of a documentary to coincide with the show's thirtieth anniversary. In 2020, during the height of the COVID-19 pandemic, fans responded to Spotnitz's challenge to write bespoke lyrics for the show's theme tune. The winning lyricists, Jennifer Large and Rebecca McDonald, saw their song recorded virtually by cast and crew from their homes, including Duchovny, Anderson, Mitch Pileggi, Robert Patrick, Annabeth Gish, and William B. Davis as well as Carter, Gilligan, Mark Snow, and Michelle MacLaren. The video, hosted on YouTube, includes a donate button to allow fans to give to the World Central Kitchen, an organization that focuses on assisting communities in crisis.

The year 2020 also saw a campaign to fund a permanent home for *The X-Files* Preservation Collection. Owned by Jim Thornton and Kelly Anthony, it is quite possibly the world's largest collection of screen-used props, wardrobe, and set dressings from the show, including furniture from Mulder's office, an alien cryopod from *Fight the Future*, the burned doll from "Chinga," and clothing worn by Mulder and Skinner. The show had already been immortalized in the Smithsonian's National Museum of American History when Carter and Spotnitz donated several items from the series to the museum's entertainment collection in 2008. These included the original, annotated pilot script, an alien maquette statue, Scully's cross necklace, the stiletto blade weapon used to kill the alien bounty hunters, the original "I Want to Believe" poster that hung in Mulder's office, and a collection of FBI badges and business cards used in the

---

23   Jones 2012.

show. Jim and Kelly have collected far more items from the show than those held by the Smithsonian and wanted to give these a home where they could not only be preserved but where other fans could visit and see the items behind the episodes. Their campaign to raise $8,000 to secure a location for the collection in Saratoga Springs, New York, was successful, and the museum opened in April 2022 with a ceremony that featured Carter and regular guest star Keith Arbuthnot. The collection features scores of items donated by Carter, including the laptop he used to write the pilot. When he originally found out about the collection, Carter wasn't sure it would ever happen, telling *Fangoria*, "It was just one of those things that felt like a pipe dream. It felt like someone had an idea that I loved, but I felt like it was a pipe dream."[24] On discovering that the museum was going ahead, however, Carter decided to donate some of his personal items to the collection. I followed the Preservation Collection on Facebook and remember Jim and Kelly sharing photos of the truckloads of items that they received, including framed posters and artwork, script cards, promotional artwork from Fox's marketing department, and behind-the-scenes film negatives. The Preservation Collection has, in addition to the physical museum, a website on which it hosts an ongoing series featuring interviews with crew members like Carter, Spotnitz, and Rob Bowman; actors such as Karin Konoval and Dean Aylesworth; and other fans who collect *X-Files*-related collectibles and memorabilia.

XXX

These new fan organizations are testament to the fact that there is still an appetite for and appreciation of the show even thirty years after it first began to air. *I Want to Believe* had sparked a renewed interest in the show in 2008, with a score of podcasts about the series popping up, including *X-Philes on File*, which began in April 2008; *Re-Opening The X-Files Podcast*, which first aired in August 2008; and the XFN

---

24   Wax. 2022. "Inside the Grand Opening of *The X-Files* Preservation Collection." *Fangoria*.

podcast, which—appropriately, given it's Carter's birthday and the name of his production company—began airing on October 13, 2009. Speculation about the revival series led to another round of podcasts appearing, including, perhaps most famously, *The X-Files Files*, hosted by actor Kumail Nanjiani, a fan of the show. Nanjiani recorded fifty-seven episodes of the podcast, in which he discussed favorite episodes and introduced guests including Darin Morgan (who subsequently invited Nanjiani to appear in his season ten episode). While many of the podcasts that sprung up in the wake of the announcement of the revival seasons have since fizzled out, *The X-Cast: An X-Files Podcast* is still going strong. The podcast began at the end of 2015, after the announcement that season ten would air early the following year. Initially, host Tony Black went through each episode chronologically while simultaneously examining season ten as it aired, but the podcast has since grown to cover the entire series run, raised almost £1,000 for charity by completing a twenty-four-hour live show, and special guests like Annabeth Gish, William B. Davis, Dean Haglund, Frank Spotnitz, Mark Snow, and comics writer Joe Harris.

The grand opening of *The X-Files* Preservation Collection was followed by an *X-Files* Fan Fest at the museum in October 2022, which included celebrity guests Nicholas Lea, the Enigma Lise, and Jenny-Lynn Hutcheson, best known as Polly from "Chinga." Several events were also planned to celebrate the show's thirtieth anniversary in 2023, including a screening of the pilot followed by a Q & A with Chris Carter at the London Science Museum, an *X-Files* 30th Anniversary Fan Fest at the *X-Files* Preservation Collection, and Phile Fest, a three-day convention organized by Off Brand Events. Judging from the discussions taking place on social media, these events were going to be well attended, with interest in the franchise from fans showing no signs of diminishing. What the future holds for the show is to be decided by Disney and Ten Thirteen, but the fandom seems likely to continue. Whether that takes the form of writing more fan fiction to "fix when Chris Carter has damaged"—as one fan told me—continuing to take part in fundraising efforts for charity, or talking about the series in online spaces, the show's fan community remains as much a part of *The X-Files* now as it did in the beginning.

CONCLUSION

Thirty Years of The X-Files

"Back in the day? Back in the day is now."
– Mulder ("Home Again")

I opened this book with a quote from season nine, and it seems fitting that I close it with a quote from one of the new seasons. The quote that opens this chapter comes from season ten's "Home Again." Mulder and Scully chase a suspect into a warehouse in search of a street artist referred to as Trashman. After telling them that the power's out, he gives the agents the slip, leaving them to descend the stairs in the dark as this exchange takes place:

> MULDER: What? I wasn't gonna shoot the kid. And I don't do stairs anymore.
> SCULLY: Mulder, back in the day, I used to do stairs. And in three-inch heels.
> MULDER: "Back in the day." Scully, back in the day [he turns on his flashlight] is now.

This scene is obviously designed to appeal to fans, but this piece of dialogue actually works on several levels. First and most obviously, it makes us think of the original series—the dark and moody setting takes us back to the Vancouver of the early seasons; the flashlights serving as one of the most iconic symbols of the show (they're even included in the opening credit sequence); the reference to Scully's heels a call back to the scene in "Hollywood A. D." when Tea Leoni asks Scully to show her how to run in high heels, itself a reference to the difference in height between Anderson and Duchovny (proving that *The X-Files* is as meta as ever). Second, it shows us how time has moved on. Mulder and Scully (and Duchovny and Anderson) perhaps aren't as spry as they used to be, and they also have to contend with new politics and technologies. And finally, it brings the show into the present day. Mulder and Scully are still doing stairs, investigating inexplicable events, and searching for the truth. The things they were doing "back in the day" are the things they're still doing now. Back in the day is no longer 1993 or 2002; it's 2016. But I think we can also see this as a subtle jab against accusations the series wouldn't be suited to the twenty-first century and was just an appeal to nostalgia.

When Fox confirmed that *The X-Files* would return to our television screens, there were concerns that it was just a cynical, money-grabbing ploy. The 2010s had already seen a slew of old(er) TV shows rebooted and revived. Among others, *Full House* (1987), *Heroes* (2006), and *24* (2001) were brought back to our screens as *Fuller House* (2016), *Heroes Reborn* (2015), and *24: Live Another Day* (2014), and news that a new season of *Twin Peaks* would air made headlines in late 2014. Nostalgia was big news in the mid-2010s, and it had proved to be a successful way to make money—bringing back beloved shows and films meant networks could draw on preexisting audiences that would not only watch them but buy the merchandise as well. Some fans worried that this wasn't a good enough reason to bring *The X-Files* back; one suggested that "Fox is reviving the show solely to increase the market value of the rights to re-air earlier episodes," while another wrote, "I worry that while it makes money, it will be dragged out for numerous seasons and therefore the quality will suffer." Many of the fans who responded to my questionnaire before season ten aired reflected on the role nostalgia played in the decision to revive the show and their responses to the news. One of the questions I asked was "How did you feel when rumors started circulating about the show's return?" Responses were mixed. One fan wrote, "I realize that a great deal of my fondness for the revival is nostalgia for the early seasons of the show, and the friends I shared the experience of the show with," while another said, "I understand the incentive to keep a popular, money-making show going in any way they can. I've just seen it happen too many times that a revived show doesn't have the same something that made it so great in the first place; they mostly sail along on audience goodwill and nostalgia." As I've shown throughout this book, however, *The X-Files* was particularly good at tapping into the dominant cultural concerns of the time in which it existed. The show holds a mirror up to the real world, be it Watergate, fake news, or any of the other issues unfolding in its time, and reflects the big questions about truth through a lens of alien abduction and shadowy governments. In that respect, it's still very much a show of its time, updated for the twenty-first century yet still asking those fundamental questions.

In this book, I've highlighted what *The X-Files* can tell us about the world we live in and how it reflects our anxieties and uncertainties. I quoted Charles Taylor in Chapter One, who argued that what linked the show to the zeitgeist in the 1990s was that Mulder and Scully were "working to get out from under the most enduring legacy of the Regan/Bush era: the way government proclaims [. . .] that the truth is irrelevant."[1] What links *The X-Files* to the zeitgeist in the 2010s is that Mulder and Scully are brought back to the FBI to investigate the truth while we're living in a post-truth age. This political and cultural climate was certainly a key inspiration for the revival seasons, although Carter says, "I don't think Mulder and Scully adopt any political position so much as a new approach in their search for the truth."[2] In an interview about the show's eleventh season, Darin Morgan suggested that it explores the boom in, and extent of, conspiracy theories saying, "This season has addressed the fact that Mulder was sort of an outcast when we originally did it, and now the conspiracy theories that are out there are too crazy even for him. There are certain theories Mulder would

---

1 Taylor 1994.

2 Hibberd 2016.

never believe for a second that are now entertained in the mainstream media."[3] Fans were, on the whole, keen to see how the show would adapt to this changing landscape; one told me they were looking forward to seeing how Carter would "reconcile with the post-90s governmental paranoia that has provided a fertile ground for profoundly damaging real-world conspiracy theories to flourish." Although conspiracies like the 9/11 truther movement (discussed in Chapter Two) had emerged early on in the twenty-first century, others have grown thanks to the rise in social media use and have made their way into the mainstream media thanks to how quickly the stories become viral online, and the revival seasons of *The X-Files* reflect that. Fox created a cult hit in the early days of the show and Carter was open to expanding the series beyond the television screen, but the fact that the show has continued to deal with the big questions of its day is one of the reasons why the revival was given the green light. Despite the—valid—criticisms that have been leveled at *The X-Files*, there's no doubt that the series has always focused on the issues that concern the fundamental aspects of humanity and seems to do so with a hint of something approaching optimism. While Jose Chung might argue that we are, in the end, all alone, years later Reggie Something reminds us that we will always have our memories. That's certainly what we have as fans of the show: memories of the series and the ways it matters to us, memories of the friendships we've made, and memories of the experiences we've had along the way. As I've discussed throughout this book, *The X-Files* has had as much of an impact on culture and society as society and culture has had on the show.

XXX

I said in the preface that this book was part history, part critical analysis, and part love letter, and I want to take advantage of the fact that I'm the writer of this book to dwell on that last part. I've made no secret of the fact that I'm a huge fan of *The X-Files*; I love this show and

---

3   de Souza 2018.

everyone involved in making it, despite its flaws. I've also been a part of the fandom since getting online in the late nineties. As such, both the fandom and the show mean a lot to me. I said in an earlier chapter that it's difficult to separate *The X-Files* from the fandom, and for me, that's certainly true. When I originally began watching, I knew only two other people who wanted to talk about it. One was my friend Cathy and the other my Form 3 English teacher. He introduced me to fan fiction when he gave us story prompts for our annual eisteddfod and is the person to whom this book is dedicated (I didn't know it was called fan fiction then, but the first story I ever wrote was about me, my sister, and Mulder and Scully investigating alien abductions in the woods near my school). My love for the show grew from there. I taped the episodes when they aired on the BBC and religiously cataloged the title, date, and synopsis of each in a notebook. My Christmas present off my gran one year was an official *X-Files* watch that lit up when you pressed a button on its side and membership of the official fan club (I still have all of these). When I went to university, I took my *Fight the Future* action figures, which my housemates placed in compromising positions much to my dismay,[4] and I bought a five-foot-tall cardboard cutout of season one Mulder and Scully that shipped from Germany (which, twenty years later, elicits questions from anyone who sees it in the background of a Zoom meeting).

Although I joined the BBC Cult message boards and shared fan fiction and discussions of the series there, I didn't become part of an in-person fan community until 2008. When *I Want to Believe* was announced, I joined an *X-Files* fan group on Facebook. There I met a girl called Michelle, who I found out was bidding on an eBay auction to win tickets to attend the premiere in London and meet Gillian Anderson. She'd never met me and didn't know me but for a few brief messages yet needed someone to go with and trusted me enough to pay my share of the ticket. In the same group I met someone who

---

4   I was, and still am, what's known in the fandom as a "noromo." Unlike shippers, who wanted to see a romantic relationship between Mulder and Scully, noromos opposed the idea. I always enjoyed the UST (unresolved sexual tension) but never wanted to see it become resolved sexual tension. Obviously it did.

told me I could stay with her and her friends in their hotel room at the premiere. It turns out she was from North Wales, and a couple of years later we were PhD candidates at the same university. Joining the Facebook group and meeting so many other fans at the premiere led to lifelong friendships with Philes across the globe. A few years later, I traveled to New York with two of the people I'd met at the premiere to see Duchovny star in an off-Broadway play. We stayed with a fellow fan we'd met online and met up with several others before I headed to Brooklyn to stay with a Phile I'd met through a LiveJournal *X-Files* community. As well as finding lasting friendships as a result of my involvement in *The X-Files* fandom, I rediscovered my ability to write, and my confidence in that writing. I've written thousands of words of fan fiction, from drabbles to short stories to novellas, as well as essays about various aspects of the show, some of which have ended up being included in this book. Thanks to *The X-Files* and its fandom, I applied for an MA in creative writing, which in turn led to my PhD.

The most obvious place where *The X-Files* has had an impact on my life is my career. While I had always wanted to write a book about the show, it felt a bit like a pipe dream. But without the show, I literally wouldn't be where I am now. If I'd never watched *The X-Files*, I'd have never become involved in the fandom, wouldn't have earned my MA, wouldn't have become interested in the ways fans rewrite issues of gender in fan fiction, wouldn't have developed that work into research on anti-fandom[5] and dislike, wouldn't have written articles about fan activism or the return of the show. I owe an incredible amount to *The X-Files* and everyone who worked on it as well as the fandom and the friends I've made along the way. So when the show came back, I dove in headfirst, and I loved it. Yes, there was exposition (but all Carter-penned episodes have had exposition), but seeing Mulder and Scully back on our screens for the first time in years was enough for me to forgive that. And I was watching it live with fans who were just

---

5   Anti-fandom as a term was first proposed by Jonathan Gray in a 2003 journal article. Initially anti-fandom referred to people who hate or dislike a show, celebrity, book, or genre, etc., but its meaning has expanded over time to include those who deliberately hate-watch or hate-read a show or book, those who create and share works that mock the text, and those who target the people involved in creating the hated text on social media.

as excited as I was. I was tweeting my friends, friends I had because of this show, sharing GIFs and memes and capslocking every other sentence. It was perfect.

XXX

Of course, fans are still making, and consuming, content about the show, and *The X-Files* remains a cultural touchstone even five years after season eleven aired. Carter was asked for his opinion on a US government report into Unidentified Aerial Phenomena in June 2021, and scores of articles about the COVID-19 conspiracy theories referred to the show, despite the lack of extraterrestrial involvement in those vaccinations. But after the season eleven finale, what of the future of the show? Anderson announced at New York Comic Con in 2017 that season eleven would be the final season of *The X-Files* for her and suggested in interviews following the finale that in order for her to consider returning the show would need to feel new: "It just feels like such an old idea. I've done it, I did it for so many years, and it also ended on such an unfortunate note. In order to even begin to have that conversation there would need to be a whole new set of writers, and the baton would need to be handed on for it to feel like it was new and progressive. So yeah, it's very much in the past."[6] While Anderson may not have been happy with the way the show was produced or how the season ended, as discussed in the last chapter, Carter seemed willing to bring the show back again. Speaking to *Digital*, he said, "I think that certainly *The X-Files* has more life in it, there are more stories to tell, with Gillian or without. I'm sorry to see her go, I've never actually considered doing this show without her, so is this the end? It's the end of something, I don't know if it's the beginning of something new."[7] For many fans, however, *The X-Files* without Scully is unthinkable. Seasons eight and nine faltered without

---

6   Zilko. 2021. "Gillian Anderson Discusses *X-Files* Sexism, Would Only Consider Revival with 'a Whole New Set of Writers.'" *IndieWire*.

7   Missim. 2018. "*X-Files*' Chris Carter interview: '*The X-Files* has more life in it–with or without Gillian Anderson.'" *Digital Spy*.

Mulder, and given the importance of the two characters to the show, it seems difficult to imagine a twelfth season succeeding with one of them missing. Of course, considering *The X-Files* as a franchise rather than a single television show means that there might be other ways to tell the stories. Carter pointed out that "you look at any long-lived franchise, and there are endless possibilities. There are prequels, there are other ways to approach a series like *The X-Files*."[8] Based on the multiple books, comics, video games, and films that emerged in the show's history, this is a valid—though perhaps not popular—point.

While for most people *The X-Files* is and always will be a televisual text featuring Anderson and Duchovny, its long and continuing history in other media does suggest the franchise might continue. As Duchovny said when asked about continuing without Anderson, "I will say this, and I mean this in all honesty, that *The X-Files* is a frame. It's a show. It happens to have these three actors in it that people have become attached to, but I believe that [the show] as a frame is completely legitimate in any form. So whether it can go on, who knows?"[9] In fact, in 2020 it was announced that an animated spinoff was in the works. Titled *The X-Files: Albuquerque* and with Carter onboard as executive producer, the cartoon would revolve around a group of FBI agents investigating cases that were too ridiculous for Mulder and Scully to focus on. While Carter confirmed at a Q & A at *The X-Files* Preservation Collection that the spinoff wouldn't be going ahead, he did tell fans following a screening of the pilot episode at the Science Museum in 2023 that Disney had approached him regarding a reboot of the show with a more diverse cast. The possibilities for developing the franchise in different ways, and beyond the characters of Mulder and Scully, remain—and might even be encouraged given *The X-Files* is now owned by Disney. The company acquired Fox's entertainment arm in March 2019. Seven years earlier, it had acquired Lucasfilm, and under Disney, five more *Star Wars* films have

8   Roffman. 2018. "'*The X-Files*' Creator Chris Carter on That Finale and the Show's Future (Without Gillian Anderson)." *The Hollywood Reporter*.

9   Easton. 2018. "Mystery Swirls for David Duchovny and Gillian Anderson Over *The X-Files* Future." *Inside Hook*.

been produced, along with several animated and live-action television series, which are available on Disney's streaming service. While *The X-Files* as a franchise isn't as big as *Star Wars*, it does have a history of working across different media, and Carter in fact announced at the same Q & A, that Disney had asked him if he would meet a *Star Wars* writer who had an idea for an *X-Files* novel. They met, and Carter was impressed with the pitch, suggesting that a new novel set in the *X-Files* universe and approved by Disney and Ten Thirteen might be on the way.

Whatever happens with the franchise, the fans are still out there. In addition to the organized fan groups and organizations I've mentioned, scores of people discuss the show on social media every day. The Reddit *X-Files* community has over 84,000 members, and recent discussion topics include events planned to celebrate the show's thirtieth anniversary, episode recaps, and questions from new viewers about the show, the mytharc, and the characters. On Facebook, the show's official page has 1.8 million followers who comment on, like, and share the frequent posts about the show. Despite there being no new installments since 2018, fans comment on past episodes, discuss the characters, and even call for new episodes. There are hundreds of fan-created pages and groups featuring everything from *X-Files* collectibles to the games (card and PC) and Duchovny and Anderson. That these groups still exist and attract new members speaks to the enduring appeal of the show. Although the interest in UFOs and abductions that permeated much of the 1990s seems to have been replaced by an all-too earthly distrust in authority, the series still speaks to fundamental ideas about faith, authority, and truth. Over the course of this book, I've tried to show how *The X-Files* spoke to the big ideas of its time, from questioning the role of AI to addressing gender disparity and pointing out the dangers of power gone unchecked. It wasn't always successful. As Scully tells Clyde Bruckman, "There are hits and there are misses. And then there are misses." *The X-Files* had its misses. But its hits showed what television could do at a time when the medium was moving into its own, and its legacy will continue well beyond its thirtieth anniversary.

Acknowledgments

When you've been part of a fandom for decades, you inevitably find yourself shaped by the people you meet and the discussions you have. Ever since I discovered the BBC Cult message boards and progressing through my involvement in fan fiction communities on LiveJournal and membership in various *The X-Files* Facebook groups, I have spent hours discussing the show, writing and reading fan fiction, and watching fan videos. I have argued about real-person fiction, shared my journey as a PhD candidate researching *The X-Files* and its fandom, and hosted rewatches and fan fiction exchanges. I'm grateful to the people I've met along the way, some of whom have become lifelong friends, and to the fans I never got to know but who still gave their time to answer survey questions and interview requests and granted permission to use their words.

I have shared early versions of the ideas explored in this book at a range of conferences, including the Genre/Nostalgia Conference at the University of Hertfordshire, the Ageing Celebrities and Ageing Fans in Popular Media Culture conference at the University of Copenhagen and the Cult Cinema and Technological Change conference at University of Aberystwyth. My thanks go to the organizers of these conferences for accepting my ideas about the show and for their support in taking those ideas further. Working in fan studies for over a decade, I have been fortunate to meet—and become friends with— enthusiastic, passionate, and welcoming scholars who have helped me shape my ideas. I'm grateful to Bertha Chin, Rebecca Williams, and Ross Garner for giving me advice, encouragement, suggestions, and *X-Files*-related GIFs. That they believe in me, and this work, means more than they'll ever know.

This book has been a labor of love and I must thank my family for being there for all of it: my dad for the cwtches, my mother for all the questions, my stepfather for reminding me to take a break, my sister Sarah for her unrelenting love and belief in me, and Loki and Milo for being my two in five billion. Elly Norman, Stephanie Thomas, Jenna Measday, Andrew Norman, Joel Weekes, and José Medina have been my constants and touchstones, and I'm lucky to have them in my life.

I am grateful to Fayetteville Mafia Press and my editors David Bushman and Scott Ryan for taking a chance on me and this book. Their comments and support throughout the writing and editing process have been incredibly helpful.

And finally, I must thank Chris Carter for creating this show in the first place. I don't know what my life would have been like without it.

Earlier versions of some of the sections and ideas in this book have been previously published elsewhere, including my LiveJournal and WordPress blogs. I would like to thank and acknowledge the editors and publishers of the following articles and chapters:

"Being of Service: *X-Files* Fans and Social Engagement." In "Transformative Works and Fan Activism," edited by Henry Jenkins and Sangita Shresthova, special issue, *Transformative Works and Cultures*, no. 10. 2012.

"The Fandom Is Out There: Social Media and *The X-Files* Online" in Kristin M. Barton and Jonathan Malcolm Lampley (eds) *Fan CULTure: Essays on participatory fandom in the 21st century*, McFarland. 2013, pp. 92-105.

"The G-Woman and The Fowl One: Fic and Femslash in *The X-Files* Fandom" in Anne Jamison (ed) *Fic: Why Fanfiction is Taking Over the World*. Smart Pop Books. 2014, pp. 116-123.

"Reopening *The X-Files*: Generational Fandom, Gender, and Bodily Autonomy," in Bridget Kies and Megan Connor (eds.) *Fandom The Next Generation*. University of Iowa Press. 2022, pp. 20-31.

"'You believe what you want to believe—that's what everybody does now': *The X-Files*, fake news and the rise of QAnon" in Diane Rodgers and James Fenwick, J. *The Legacy of The X-Files*. Bloomsbury. Forthcoming.

Bibliography

Alexander, John. *The Films of David Lynch*. London: Charles Letts, 1993.

Arras, Paul. 2018. *The Lonely Nineties*. Visions of Community in Contemporary US Television. Springer International Publishing.

Badley, Linda. 2000. "Scully Hits the Glass Ceiling: Postmodernism, Postfeminism, Posthumanism, and *The X-Files*" in Elyce Rae Helford (ed), *Fantasy Girls: Gender in the New Universe of Science Fiction and Fantasy Television*. Rowman & Littlefield, pp. 61-90.

Bellon, Joe. 1999. "The strange discourse of *The X-Files*: What it is, what it does, and what is at stake." *Critical Studies in Media Communication* 16.2, pp. 136-154.

Brinker, Felix. 2018. "Conspiracy, Procedure, Continuity: Reopening *The X-Files*", *Television & New Media*, Vol. 19(4), pp. 328–344.

Cantor, Paul A. 2012. *The Invisible Hand in Popular Culture: Liberty Vs. Authority in American Film and TV*. The University Press of Kentucky.

Carter, Chris. 2008. "A Word With Chris Carter." *The X-Files* #0. *Wildstorm Comics*.

Crang, M. A. 2015. *Denying the Truth: Revisiting The X-Files after 9/11*. CreateSpace Independent Publishing Platform.

d'Ancona, Matthew. 2017. *Post-Truth: The New War on Truth and How to Fight Back*. Ebury Press.

Davies, Jason. 2016. *Writing The X-Files. Interviews with Chris Carter, Frank Spotnitz, Vince Gilligan, John Shiban and Howard Gordon*. HarlanEllisonBooks. com.

Delasara, Jan. 2000. *Poplit, Popcult and the X Files: A Critical Explanation: A Critical Exploration*. McFarland.

Donaldson, Amy M. 2007. "The Last Temptation of Mulder: Reading *The X-Files* through the Christological Lens of Nikos Kazantzakis" in Sharon R. Yang (ed.) *The X-files and Literature: Unweaving the Story, Unraveling the Lie to Find the Truth*. Cambridge Scholars, pp. 2-29.

Geraghty, Lincoln. 2014. *Cult Collectors*. Routledge

Goldman, Jane. 1996. *The X-Files Book of the Unexplained, Volume II*. New York: Harper Prism.

Graham, Allison. 1996. "'Are You Now or Have You Ever Been?' Conspiracy Theory and *The X-Files*", in David Lavery, Angela Hague and Marla Cartwright (eds.), *Deny All Knowledge: Reading The X-Files*, 52-62. London: Faber and Faber.

Gray, Jonathan. 2003. "New audiences, new textualities: Anti-fans and non-fans." *International journal of cultural studies*, 6(1), pp.64-81.

Gulyas, Aaron John. 2015. *The Paranormal and the Paranoid: Conspiratorial Science Fiction Television*. Rowman & Littlefield.

Haggins, Bambi L. "Apocrypha Meets the Pentagon Papers: The Appeals of *The X-Files* to the X-Phile." *Journal of Film and Video* 53:4 (2002) pp. 8-28.

Haggins, Bambi and Julia Himberg. 2018. "The Multi-Channel Transition Period, 1980s–1990s." In Aniko Bodroghkozy (ed) A Companion to American Broadcasting. John Wiley & Sons, pp. 111-133.

Handlen, Zak and Emily Todd Vanderwerff. 2018. Monsters of the Week The Complete Critical Companion to *The X-Files*. Abrams Press

Hansen, Regina. "Catholicism in *The X-Files*: Dana Scully and the harmony of faith and reason." *Science Fiction Film and Television* 6.1 (2013) pp. 55-69.

Hassler-Forest, Dan. 2020. "When you get there, you will already be there': *Stranger Things, Twin Peaks* and the nostalgia industry', *Science Fiction Film and Television* 13.2, pp. 175–97.

Helford, Elyce Rae. 2000. *Fantasy Girls: Gender in the New Universe of Science Fiction and Fantasy Television*. Rowman & Littlefield.

Hill, Rodney F. ""I Want to Believe the Truth Is Out There": *The X-Files* and the Impossibility of Knowing." *Science Fiction Film, Television, and Adaptation*. Routledge, 2011, pp. 145-156.

Hodges, Lacy. 2005. *"Scully, What Are You Wearing?": The Problem of Feminism, Subversion, and Heteronormativity in The X-Files*. MA Diss. University of Florida.

Howell, Amanda. 2000. "*The X-Files*, X-Philes and X-Philia: Internet fandom as a site of convergence." *Media International Australia* 97, no. 1, pp. 137-149.

Howley, Kevin. 2001. "Spooks, Spies, and Control Technologies in *The X-Files*." *Television & New Media*, 2(3), pp. 257–280.

Hurwitz, Matt and Knowles, Chris. 2008. *The Complete X-Files. Insight Editions*.

Hurwitz, Matt and Knowles, Chris. 2016. *The Complete X-Files Revised and Updated Edition*. Insight Editions.

Inness, Sherrie A. 1999. *Tough Girls: Women Warriors and Wonder Women in Popular Culture*. University of Pennsylvania Press.

Jacobs, Stephen, Geoffery Long, Kathering Isbister, and Richard Rouse III. 2006. "Occasionally reconcilable differences: bringing games and linear entertainment IP together, for better and for worse." In *Proceedings of the 2006 ACM SIGGRAPH symposium on Videogames*, pp. 13-17.

Jenkins, Henry. 1992. *Textual Poachers: Television, Fans and Participatory Culture*. New York: Routledge.

Jenkins, Henry. 2006. *Convergence Culture: Where Old and New Media Collide*. NYU Press.

Johnson, Catherine. 2005. 'Quality/Cult Television: *The X-Files* and Television History' in Michael Hammond, and Lucy Mazdon (eds) *The Contemporary Television Series*. Edinburgh University Press, pp. 57-74..

Johnson, Derek. 2007. "Inviting audiences in: The spatial reorganization of production and consumption in 'TVIII'." *New Review of Film and Television Studies* 5, no. 1, pp. 61-80.

Jones, Bethan. 2012. "Being of service: *X-Files* fans and social engagement." In Henry Jenkins and Sangita Shresthova (eds) "Transformative Works and Fan

Activism," special issue, *Transformative Works and Cultures*, 10.

Jones, Bethan. 2013a. "The Fandom Is Out There: Social Media and *The X-Files* Online" in Kristin M. Barton and Jonathan Malcolm Lampley (eds) *Fan CULTure: Essays on participatory fandom in the 21st century*, McFarland pp. 92-105.

Jones, Bethan. 2013b. "Mulder/Scully versus the G-Woman and the Fowl One" in Anne Jaminson (ed) *Fic: Why Fanfiction Is Taking Over the World*, Smart Pop pp. 116-123.

Kackman, Michael. 2018. "Television Before the Classic Network Era: 1930s-1950s." In Aniko Bodroghkozy (ed) A Companion to American Broadcasting. John Wiley & Sons, pp.71-91.

Kellner, Douglas. 1999. "*The X-Files* and the aesthetics and politics of postmodern pop." *Journal of Aesthetics and Art Criticism* 57 (2) pp. 161-175

Kessenich, Tom. 2002. *Examination: An Unauthorized Look at Seasons 6–9 of The X-Files*. Trafford Publishing.

Kimmell, Daniel M. 2004. The Fourth Network: How Fox Broke the Rules and Reinvented Television. Ivan R. Dee.

Kompare, Derek. 2006. "Publishing Flow: DVD Box Sets and the Reconception of Television." *Television & New Media*, 7(4), pp. 335–360.

Kowalski, Dean. 2007. *The Philosophy of The X-Files*. The University Press of Kentucky

Lavery, David, Hague, Angela and Cartwright, Maria. 1996. *Deny All Knowledge: Reading the "X-Files"*. Faber and Faber

Lotz, Amanda D. 2009. "What is US television now?." *The annals of the American academy of political and social science* 625.1, pp. 49-59.

Lovece, Frank. 1996. *The X-Files Declassified*. Citadel Press.

Lowry, Brian. 1995. *The Truth Is Out There: The Official Guide To The X-Files*. New York: Harper Collins.

Lowry, Brian. 1996. *Trust No One: The Official Third Season Guide to The X Files*. New York: Harper Collins.

McCarthy, Donald. 2017. "How Twin Peaks Brought Viewers Existential Mobsters and Advertising Doppelgängers." In Eric Hoffman and Dominick Grace (eds) *Approaching Twin Peaks Critical Essays on the Original Series*. McFarland, pp. 154-167.

Meisler, Andy. 1999. *Resist or Serve: The Official Guide to The X-Files*, Vol. 4, London: HarperCollins.

Meisler, Andy. 2000. *The End and the Beginning: The Official Guide to The X-Files Season 6*. HarperCollins.

Mittell, Jason. 2015. *Complex TV: The poetics of contemporary television storytelling*. NYU Press.

Mooney, Darren. 2017. *Opening The X-Files: A Critical History of the Original Series*. McFarland.

Nera Kera, Myrto Pantazi and Oliver Klein. 2018. "These Are Just Stories, Mulder": Exposure to Conspiracist Fiction Does Not Produce Narrative Persuasion." *Frontiers in Psychology*. Volume 9, article 684, pp. 1-17.

Petrucha, Stephen. 1994. "Welcome to *The X-Files* Comic." *The X-Files* Issue #1, pp. 29-30. *Topps Comics*.

Perron, Bernard, Dominic Arsenault, Martin Picard, and Carl Therrien. 2008. "Methodological questions in 'interactive film studies'." *New Review of Film and Television Studies 6*, no. 3, pp.233-252.

Picarelli, Enrica and M. Carmen Gomez-Galisteo. 2013. "Be fearful: *The X-Files'* post-9/11 legacy." *Science Fiction Film and Television*, 6(1), pp. 71-85.

Pillai, Nicolas. 2013. 'What am I looking at, Mulder?': Licensed comics and the freedoms of transmedia storytelling. *Science Fiction Film and Television*, 6(1), pp.101-117.

Reeves, Jimmie L., Rodgers, Mark C and Epstein, Michael. 1996. "Rewriting Popularity: The Cult Files." In David Lavery, Angela Hague and Marla Cartwright (eds) *Deny All Knowledge: Reading The X-Files*. London: Faber and Faber, pp. 22-35.

Regan-Wills, Emily. 2013. "Fannish discourse communities and the construction of gender in *The X-Files*." *Transformative Works and Cultures*, 14.

Rumbaugh, Gina Boyer. 2008. *X-chromosomes within The X-Files: An Examination of Celebrity Role Models Agent Scully and Gillian Anderson*. VDM Verlag Dr. Muller Aktiengesellschaft & Co. KG.

Scodari, Christina., and Felder, Jenna, L. 2000. "Creating a pocket universe: "Shippers," fan fiction, and *The X-Files* Online." *Communication Studies: 51* (3), pp. 238-257.

Shapiro, Marc. 2000. *All Things: The Official Guide to The X-Files Volume 6*. Harper Prism.

Shearman, Robert. 2009. *Wanting to Believe: A Critical Guide to The X-Files, Millennium & The Lone Gunmen*. Mad Norwegian Press.

Short, Sue. 2011. *Cult Telefantasy Series: A Critical Analysis of The Prisoner, Twin Peaks, The X-Files, Buffy the Vampire Slayer, Lost, Heroes, Doctor Who and Star Trek* (Vol. 30). McFarland.

Soter, Tom. 2015. *Investigating Couples: A Critical Analysis of The Thin Man, The Avengers and The X-Files*. McFarland.

Taylor, Charles. 1994. "Truth Decay: Sleuths after Reagan." *Millennium Pop* 1.1

Tooze, Adam. 2018. *Crashed: How a Decade of Financial Crises Changed the World*. Penguin.

Vitaris, Paula. 1995. "*X-Files*: Pushing Horror's Envelope. *Cinefantastique*, Vol 26 no. 6/Vol 27 no.1.

Von Kallenbach, Gareth. 2004. *Skiewed and Reviewed 2004 Back for More*. Lulu Press, Incorporated.

Zimmerman, Dwight Jon. 1995. "The Making of *The X-Files* Comic Book Series." *The X-Files* Issue #0, pp. 47-48. *Topps Comics*.

For more detail on website articles used, go to ScottRyanProductions.com

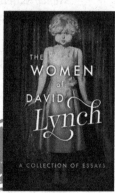
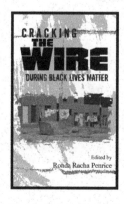

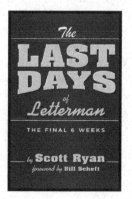

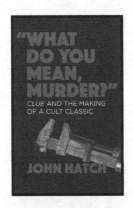

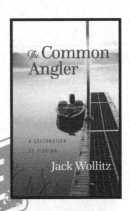
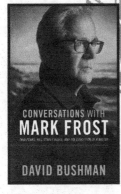